ADVANCE PRAISE FOR
THE POWER OF CHARACTER STRENGTHS

Finally, Ryan Niemiec and Bob McGrath—who have been on the frontlines of our understanding of how to nurture the best within us—wrote this much-needed book! This is the most scientifically valid and useful book on character strengths to date. The focus on 24 character strengths is highly accessible and of benefit for anyone—young, old, professional, self-employed, unemployed, student, or military—who wants to better understand their potential and learn concrete strategies to bring out the best in themselves and others.

> —Scott Barry Kaufman, Ph.D., Author of *Ungifted: Intelligence Redefined* and Co-Author of *Wired to Create: Unraveling the Mysteries of the Creative Mind*

The authors offer a crucially-needed roadmap to thriving and living life to the fullest, offering an alternative to focusing on faults, flaws and failings.

> —Sandra Scheinbaum, Ph.D., IFMCP
> Founder and CEO, Functional Medicine Coaching Academy, Inc.

Did you know you have a way within you to discover all that is good and right about yourself? It is mind-expanding and life enhancing! After you discover your strengths with the VIA Survey, use this book as the framework for a fun, doable, and mind-blowing recipe for how you can begin to shine a positivity light on your life right now!

> —Judy Krings, coach and psychologist

I was diagnosed with invasive breast cancer at the age of 34. I have no family history (of any cancer!). I was a Division I athlete, maintained an active lifestyle, and was otherwise extremely healthy. Knowing my strengths before this "detour" allowed me to know what I should focus on each day. These character strengths practices have kept me on a path of resilience and happiness throughout my diagnosis and treatment.

—Lani Silversides, Mathematics Instructor and athletic coach at Phillips Academy Andover,
Certified Sport Psychology Coach, and Certified Positive Educator

Drs. Niemiec and McGrath, the preeminent scholars and practitioners of character strengths development, have helped me deeply understand and deploy my signature strengths of love of learning, curiosity and zest, enabling me to thrive in both my professional and home life. I strongly recommend their exceptional new book—*The Power of Character Strengths*. This magnificent guide sparkles with essential knowledge and practical tips, plus the included four-step Strengths Builder program will definitely boost your career success, happiness and life satisfaction.

—Jeffrey E. Auerbach, Ph.D.,
President, College of Executive Coaching; Co-Author of *Positive Psychology in Coaching*

As a strengths-based psychotherapist, this work with character strengths has profoundly changed the way my clients see themselves and the kind of work we do together.

—Jennifer Cory, MS, MAPP, LCSW
Clinical Psychotherapist and Founder HEART Initiative

Here is a book that can change your life like it did mine.

—Kristen Carter, Positive Psychology Coach and Writer

An Official Guide from the VIA Institute on Character

THE **POWER**
OF CHARACTER
STRENGTHS

APPRECIATE and **IGNITE**
Your Positive Personality

Ryan M. Niemiec & Robert E. McGrath

VIA Classification of Character Strengths and Virtues*

Virtue of Wisdom

- **Creativity:** Original and adaptive, shows ingenuity, sees and does things in different ways
- **Curiosity:** Interested, seeks novelty, appreciates exploration, open to experience
- **Judgment:/Critical Thinking:** thinks through all sides, doesn't jump to conclusions
- **Love of Learning:** Interested in mastering new skills and information, systematically adds to knowledge
- **Perspective:** Wise, provides wise counsel, takes the big-picture view

strengths that help you gather and use knowledge

Virtue of Courage

- **Bravery:** Shows valor, doesn't shrink from threat or challenge, faces fears, speaks up for what's right
- **Perseverance:** Persistent, industrious, finishes what he or she starts, overcomes obstacles
- **Honesty:** Authentic, true to him- or herself, sincere, shows integrity
- **Zest:** Vital, enthusiastic for life, vigorous, energetic, does things wholeheartedly

strengths that help you exercise your will and face adversity

Virtue of Humanity

- **Love:** Both loving and loved, values close relations with others, shows genuine warmth
- **Kindness:** Generous, nurturing, caring, compassionate, altruistic, does for others
- **Social Intelligence:** Emotionally intelligent, aware of the motives and feelings of self and others, knows what makes other people tick

strengths that help you in one-on-one relationships

Virtue of Justice

- **Teamwork:** A good citizen, socially responsible, loyal, contributes to group efforts
- **Fairness:** Adheres to principles of justice, doesn't let feelings bias decisions, offers equal opportunity to all
- **Leadership:** Organizes groups to get things done, positively guides others

strengths that help you in community or group-based situations

Virtue of Temperance

- **Forgiveness:** Merciful, accepting of others' shortcomings, gives people a second chance, lets go of hurt when wronged
- **Humility:** Modest, lets his or her accomplishments speak for themselves
- **Prudence:** Careful about his or her choices, cautious, doesn't take undue risks
- **Self-Regulation:** Self-controlled; disciplined; able to manage impulses, emotions, and vices

strengths that help you manage habits and protect against excess

Virtue of Transcendence

- **Appreciation of Beauty and Excellence:** Experiences awe and wonder for beauty, admires skills and excellence in others, elevated by moral beauty (the goodness of others)
- **Gratitude:** Thankful for the good in life, expresses thanks, feels blessed
- **Hope:** Optimistic, positive and future-minded, expects the best and works to achieve it
- **Humor:** Playful, brings smiles to others, lighthearted, sees the lighter side
- **Spirituality:** Having coherent beliefs about the higher purpose and meaning of the universe, knowing where one fits within the larger scheme, having beliefs about the meaning of life that shape conduct and provide comfort

strengths that help you connect to the larger universe and provide meaning

* Virtues refer to the 6 core characteristics valued by philosophers and theologians across culture and time. Character strengths refer to the 24 positive personality ingredients of a fulfilling life, the pathways to the virtues.

Printed and bound in the United States of America
ISBN: 978-0-578-43429-2
Library of Congress Control Number: 2019931659

DEDICATED TO . . .

Danny Wedding
Who saw something unique in my character

Neal and Donna Mayerson
Who championed my character

Mom and Dad
Who allowed me to freely discover and express my character
Ryan

Deborah, Megan, and Brian
They are the ones who make me want to be a person of character
Bob

GRATITUDE

If you don't already know everything there is to know about the VIA Institute on Character, and you probably don't, we want to introduce you to this very special organization. It is not your typical nonprofit. It's rare in today's world to say that a nonprofit organization not only succeeds for a moment in time and is self-sustaining, but that it is also selfless, fully mission-driven, highly impactful, and only getting stronger each year. The VIA Institute devotes its work to advancing the science and practical applications of character strengths. As a result, every 5 seconds, someone from around the world comes to the VIA website (www.viacharacter.org) to learn more about strengths. Every 15 seconds, someone uses the website to complete VIA's free flagship questionnaire—officially named the VIA Inventory of Strengths, but informally called the VIA Survey—and receives their free character strengths survey results. These numbers have steadily increased over the last fifteen years and dramatically increased each of the last five years.

The science of character has simultaneously exploded. Not very long ago, researchers had almost nothing to say about character; today, research teams from around the globe have generated well over five hundred scientific publications about the nature of character, how to improve character, and how people can use character strengths in their daily lives. This work on the 24 character strengths of the VIA Classification, the VIA Survey, and related concepts has spurred the development of a community of practitioners who are applying principles of character in business, education, coaching, and counseling. No one has any idea how many of these strengths practitioners exist around the world, but we estimate the number is in the hundreds of thousands. This book would not have been possible without the contributions of those people, and those people's contributions would not have occurred without the work of the VIA Institute. More than anyone else, then, we want to acknowledge the hard and selfless work of the remarkable VIA Institute and its team.

All that the VIA has done can be traced back to a phone call between Neal Mayerson (VIA Chairman) and Marty Seligman (founder of positive psychology) in 1999 that began the journey to this book. Neal and Donna Mayerson have, as a duo, donated hundreds of hours of their time, sharing wisdom, experiences, and leadership to help VIA grow, never taking any personal income from the VIA Institute. On a side note, we want to give a deep bow to the Manuel D. & Rhoda Mayerson Foundation, which funded the founding of the VIA Institute and its initial work, and kept it going in the early years before VIA became self-sustaining. We also wish to acknowledge the deep debt of our entire field to the work of Chris Peterson, the original science director at the VIA Institute, who teamed with Marty to lead fifty-five scientists and found the science of character underlying VIA's work. His death in 2012 was a great loss to our field.

We also want to emphasize gratitude to core VIA team members Breta Cooper, VIA Business Director, and Kelly Aluise, VIA Communications Specialist. They're the ones who keep VIA running on a daily basis. Without them, our work would be so much more difficult, and they were essential to making this book possible.

Working with us, Breta, and Kelly on this project was project manager extraordinaire, the uniquely empowering character strengths author, Ruth Pearce. This team was involved from the book's inception to its printing, including each of the mind-boggling number of stages, challenges, and decisions that had to be made with thoughtfulness, collaboration, and vision. We also want to thank our publishing partner, Bethany Kelly, whose collaboration, creativity, and advice has been instrumental in making this book possible.

A number of people read an earlier draft of this book and offered encouragement, general feedback, and constructive criticism and ideas. We are pleased to express gratitude to Joseph Fernando Bacigalupo, Kathy Bicha, Kristen Carter, Jillian Darwish, Danny W. Futrell, Judy Krings, Helen O'Donohue, Lisa Sansom, Barbara Winwood, and Cheryl Zawacki for the thoughtfulness demonstrated in their comments.

The idea for this book was born about ten years ago when the former Executive Director of VIA, Deb Pinger, told Ryan that "we need a consumer-friendly book." He agreed, but the timing wasn't right. Over the years, many other individuals gave the same feedback, including people in the general public like Julie Wharton and leaders in the field of positive psychology like Itai Ivtzan. But the timing still wasn't right . . . until Breta and Ryan connected around the idea of VIA offering a book like this for the general consumer as part of a larger suite of VIA offerings. At almost exactly the same time, Bob independently raised exactly the same idea to Neal. Maybe this was synchronicity, maybe it was random; either way, we knew the time was right. To all of the people we've listed, thank you for your part in bringing this ten-year journey to this climax; we're deeply grateful that each one of you has been part of that journey.

Finally, we also wish to thank our other colleagues, friends, and family. We appreciate your care and support of not only our work, but of who we are.

TABLE OF CONTENTS

MEET THE AUTHORS

MEET RYAN

I am propelled by my highest strengths: **love** and **hope**. These come forth in my teaching, my work with clients and colleagues, and especially with my family. Love is the fuel that connects me with others. It drives me to be open-minded and to appreciate all of humanity. Hope is the fuel that leads me to appreciate the present moment and to strive for betterment in the future. These two strengths are particularly clear when I'm chasing my three young children around and attempting to savor every unique thing they say or do; I act as if each child was the first person to say the words, "I did it!" when turning off a light switch or "Go away, Daddy" when trying to put on their shoes independently. As I consider possibilities in the future for my work with character strengths, it is the energy of hope that orients me toward the numerous pathways by which these strengths can be used to tap into and to see the goodness in people.

1

My most obvious top strengths are probably **curiosity** and **honesty**. When I'm not lost in a project, people will observe me as asking a lot of questions and doing what I can to explore a topic. I am a constant pursuer of new experiences, traveler to new places, and consumer of new foods and collectibles. When traveling to new countries, my colleagues have commented on my curiosity about the wildlife as I try to get as close as reasonably possible to fully take in the experience. Meanwhile, honesty is integral to me. Sometimes my wife calls me "the confessor" because my truth-telling is so high that it's as if I'm saying extra information to offer the whole truth or I'm veering deep into self-disclosure. It's not that I'm not clever enough to evade the truth; it's that I choose not to. It feels to me as if that would be unfair to the other person. I know heavy doses of honesty can sometimes be risky and take me to uncomfortable places, but I believe people are strong enough to handle the truth and that they deserve that much (there's my **fairness** strength emerging too). Hopefully, most of the time, my strengths of love and hope are expressed along with honesty and fairness to not offend others.

Appreciation of beauty is a character strength most people don't know about me, and it doesn't come across in my appearance, the cars I drive, or my possessions. It comes across in my discovering beauty in the little things, in dark places, and in the mundane. I can be awe-struck by one leaf or insect, brought to tears by an act of kindness in a TV show, and marvel at the contours of a tree line or a cloud pattern in the sky.

Dr. Ryan Niemiec is the education director at the VIA Institute on Character, annual instructor at the University of Pennsylvania, adjunct professor at Xavier University, and author of several books, including *Mindfulness and Character Strengths*, *Positive Psychology at the Movies*, and *Character Strengths Interventions*. He's an award-winning psychologist and Fellow of the International Positive Psychology Association.

MEET BOB

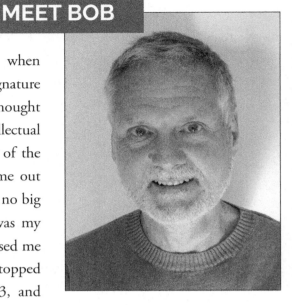

I was a little surprised when I first saw my signature strengths. I've always thought of myself as a pretty intellectual guy, so I expected some of the wisdom strengths to come out on top. Therefore, it was no big surprise that **curiosity** was my #2 strength. What confused me was finding that **bravery** topped the list, **honesty** was #3, and **zest** was #5. Three of the four **courage** strengths were in my top five! I had no idea what to make of that at first.

I've never run into a burning building to save someone, or been in a war zone. As I thought about it, though, I realized that a good deal of the growth I've experienced in my life, both personally and professionally, has come from the small risks I've taken. Looking back on my past, I realized I've frequently done things that I didn't think of as brave at the time, but they were things most people would not have done. In a family where education wasn't that highly prized, I decided at an early age that I wanted to become a psychologist, and I never wavered from that journey. I wasn't naturally the kind of person who looked closely at myself, but once I realized I had things I needed to work on as a person, I really dedicated myself to examining the kind of person I am and the kind of person I wanted to be. I think this process, which still goes on forty years later, helped me develop a more objective sense of my strengths and weaknesses. I think it also helped me become a more caring and empathic person than I would have been naturally, a better parent and a better partner.

I've also started to realize that I reach more in my career than most people. If I think there is an uncomfortable topic that needs to be addressed, I'll address it. Not long ago a colleague said to me, "You're really good at getting your foot in the door." I've had a number of experiences where I've contacted someone, even if I've never met them before, and told them why they should want to work on a project with me. It's amazing how often those contacts have paid off. I also was apologizing recently to an administrator at my university that I was trying to do something no one else at the university had ever done, and it was causing complications for his office. His response was, "You're always out ahead of everyone else here. I wish there were more like you." I still think it sounds too dramatic to refer to myself as brave. There have also been times when I have not been as honest as I should have been. That said, the VIA has helped me see how much risk-taking has been a part of who I am (though I'm pretty prudent in the risks I take—no bungee jumping for me!).

What helps these risks pay off is that **self-regulation** rounds out my top five. I'm particularly proud of that one. When I make a commitment to do something, I follow through no matter what it takes. People trust me because of it, and it's a core part of my work ethic. I've asked my students to rate what they thought were my signature strengths, and self-regulation was always on their list. That's one way in which others see me as I see myself.

Dr. Robert McGrath is Professor in and Director of the School of Psychology at Fairleigh Dickinson University. He is one of two Senior Scientists at the VIA Institute on Character. He is also the Director of

Integrated Care for the Underserved of Northeastern New Jersey, a federally funded program providing behavioral health services to low-income individuals in primary care. That program exists because once upon a time Dr. McGrath called someone he had never met at a local healthcare agency and convinced that person they should work on a project with him.

A NOTE TO THE READER

What you have in front of you is the first book of its kind. It is a book about what is best within you—your many strengths of character.

As the poet Walt Whitman once observed, "Character and personal force are the only investments that are worth anything." This book offers a recipe for that investment in yourself. You'll never regret having taken time and energy to work on personal development that helps you grow as a person and helps others.

What lies before you on these pages is nothing compared to what lies within you. It is a reflection of you and your potential. You are about to see and bring forth that potential not just for yourself but also for others. The way you use your strengths—individually and collectively—makes you unique and special. Your character strengths support you and support others. No two people use their strengths in the same way. In this book, you will find out how *you* can use your strengths to be your best self, the person you most want to be!

This book attempts to balance concepts and education with practical ideas. To make it easy to navigate, we have organized it into three sections. The first section offers an introduction to this work—its key concepts, why it's important, and why it might matter to you. The second section is the bulk of the book. We describe the what, the why, and the how of each of the 24 character strengths found by scientists in all human beings. The third section of the book emphasizes the latter as we outline *Strengths Builder*, a practical four-week program based squarely in science for boosting your character strengths to thrive in your life.

It's unlikely you'll decide to read the book cover to cover. Instead, you might read the first section and then choose the character strengths you are most curious about in the second section. Or, you might choose to look closely at each of your signature strengths as they appear in Part II. For any character strength you focus on, learn about the strength, reflect on the questions, and see yourself in the examples of everyday people. Most important, experiment with the many activities we offer. We hope you will return over and over to this second section as a resource for general strengths education, and for ideas you can build into your strengths-based practice. As we often say, all 24 character strengths matter. Each helps us in different ways as we create greater wellness, build relationships, navigate stress, and reach our goals.

After you've done some exploring, discussing, and practicing with character strengths, turn to Part III and go through the four-step *Strengths Builder* program described there closely. You might do this on your own, or even better, with others. Complete the program with your teammates or co-workers. Discuss it with your relationship partner, or your friends and family. Bring it to your neighborhood as a way to foster a stronger community. When you're ready, be sure to take action with it, reflect on the insights and positive changes you experience, and repeat it—in part or in its entirety—as often as you like.

Ultimately, give the gift of your character strengths to others by expressing them throughout your life. It is our hope that your increased use of character strengths—multiplied across each individual—will contribute to a better world.

As you read these pages and integrate strengths fully into your life journey, we hope you become as excited by character strengths as we are!

May you grow in strengths awareness.
May you appreciate, ignite, and grow your strengths use.
May your strengths benefit others.
May your life be filled with well-being.

Yours, in strength,

Ryan Niemiec and Robert McGrath

January 2019

PART I:
INTRODUCTION

You are a person of character. In fact, each of us is. Each of us has in us, to varying degrees, certain traits that are admired and respected by others. These traits are called "character strengths." For you, some may have already fully flowered, and you are expressing them strongly in your life; some of these strengths may be dormant, waiting for you to refocus your attention on them; and some may have never gotten any deliberate attention from you over the years. Wherever you stand on each of the traits of character, they are already there in you.

This is a book for people who want to learn more about character in general, and *their character* in particular, with the goal of making their lives better. It is about learning more about what defines you as a person worthy of respect, love, and appreciation, and how you can use those positive elements of who you are to improve your sense of well-being, your relationships, and even your community.

Character is the part of your personality that other people tend to admire, respect, and cherish. It is the sum total of those aspects of who you are as a person that leads others to see you as a person with integrity, a person who contributes, a person who can be trusted.

Modern research sponsored by the VIA Institute on Character has discovered that there are 24 central character strengths in human beings, each falling under larger categories called virtues. These character strengths are the positive parts of our personality, qualities like kindness, curiosity, and perseverance that are a vital part of who we are, and that are considered valuable by other people and by society as a whole. At the front of this book, you can review the full list of 24 character strengths and the virtues they fall under. This system is called the *VIA Classification of Character Strengths and Virtues*. You may wonder in some cases why a strength is with one virtue but not another. When the VIA Classification was developed, the authors realized that the connections between strengths and virtues aren't perfect. It's possible for a strength to reflect more than one virtue, and some strengths are more clearly connected to one particular virtue than another. Don't get too hung up on these associations. They're meant to give you a general sense of how strengths tend to cluster and reinforce each other.

> Character is the part of your personality that other people tend to admire, respect, and cherish.

The VIA Classification was the result of several years of research, involving more than fifty scientists, led by luminary scientists Christopher Peterson and Martin Seligman, who looked across countries and cultures for those qualities that are universally considered to be the strongest parts of being human. In addition to studying tens of thousands of people across continents, researchers went to some of the remotest places on the planet to speak with people about these strengths. For example, they spoke with members of the Maasai tribe in Kenya and Inuit in northern Greenland, places that few people have traveled to, and asked them about these character strengths: if they were valued in their culture, if there were ways to build them up, and if they were fulfilling traits. These early pioneers were learning that the character strengths were an important part of what makes us human.

As research on character strengths has flourished, a hierarchy for understanding the layout of the VIA Classification has become clearer. Consider the layout below.

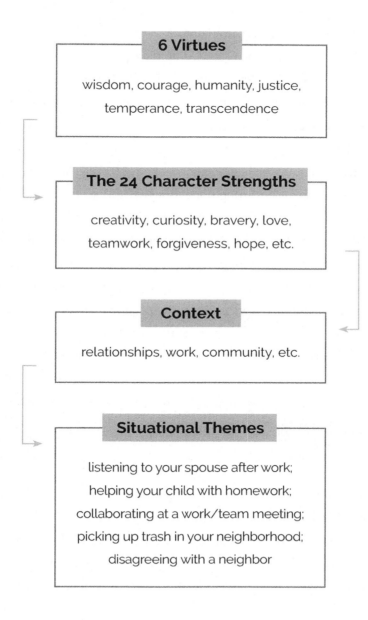

While virtues are those characteristics valued by philosophers and theologians across time, cultures, and beliefs, character strengths make up the broader categories of virtues, and are often viewed as the "routes" to the virtues of wisdom, courage, humanity, and so on. The strengths are expressed in the important areas of our life (e.g., the contexts of work, school, community, and relationships). You may use your leadership to organize a community project or your perseverance to finish a work task. Finally, within any context lies a seemingly infinite number of scenarios, or situational themes, where the character strengths are used; for example, when you are at a team meeting, talking with your boss, or helping a customer, to name a few in the work context.

Character strengths are basic elements of our identity. When we express these character strengths through our thoughts and actions, research says we tend to feel happier, more connected, and more productive. What is particularly remarkable about character strengths is that they can contribute to your personal well-being, to the quality of your relationships, and to your community as a whole. For example, your curiosity helps you explore new ideas, people, and places; your teamwork allows you to collaborate on projects and see the value of every person's contribution; and your bravery helps you move out of your comfort zone, challenging yourself and others.

> Character strengths make up the
> broader categories of virtues

It's worth noting that not every personal strength is a character strength. *Talents* like a natural ability to play music or basketball, or having good spatial or writing ability are also strengths, but they're not part of character. The foundations of talents are more hard-wired and less changeable. Character strengths are also different from our *interests* and *passions*, which engage us in topics and activities we enjoy; and they're different from *skills* we develop, such as computer skills or presentation skills. These can be important and can contribute to us and to those around us, but they need not be central to how we think of ourselves. In contrast, character strengths cut straight to the core of who we are. They reflect our basic "being" as human beings, and our "doing"—that is, the good we put out into the world.

Another way to divide the strengths instead of between the six virtues is by strengths of the head and strengths of the heart. Strengths of the head are more analytical, logic-based, and thinking-focused, such as judgment, prudence, fairness, love of learning, and perspective. Strengths of the heart are centered on our feelings, intuitions, and our emotional relationships, such as kindness, love, humor, gratitude, and spirituality. No strength falls perfectly in one category, as each has elements of head and heart. These categories refer to the direction in which the strength more strongly leans. Both the head and the heart strengths are important to our being well-rounded people, though the heart strengths in general are more reliably associated with feelings of well-being and satisfaction.

Why Should I Care About Character Strengths?

This is an important question to understand. First, we'll answer it through the experiences of Hannah B.

Hannah, a middle-aged, married woman with two children, felt like things were slipping in her life, slipping out of control. Her work as a fashion designer felt boring and meaningless. Her two boys were becoming more and more independent by the day, with little interest in the "mother-son" bonding that she used to cherish. The intimacy in her marriage was lost, and she and her husband seemed to be barely passing by each other at home amidst their busy lifestyle. Generally, Hannah felt pretty down, sometimes anxious, sometimes distracted, and generally disconnected from her life. It was as if she was going through the motions, merely a passive participant in her life. She had felt this way for several years, ever since her mother suddenly passed away. One of the upsides for Hannah was the two or three close friends with whom she had coffee every couple of weeks.

One day, while sipping a latte, her friend suggested Hannah might take a test that would tell her about her best qualities. "I already know that about me" was Hannah's response. Her friend persisted, and Hannah's reluctance turned into resignation: "OK, I'll do it," she promised as they parted ways. That evening, Hannah kept her promise and took the online VIA Survey to assess her character strengths. She wasn't expecting much as she absentmindedly printed out her results. After a moment, she glanced down at the page and did a double take as she looked more closely at her top strengths of character.

She read them one by one. Kindness. Gratitude. Honesty. Curiosity. Humor. "That's me?" she wondered aloud, with a mixture of excitement, surprise, and intrigue. She thought for a moment as she read the descriptions of each strength. It was in that instant that Hannah realized something: "I want to get my life back. No—I'm going to get my life back. And now I know how!"

Hannah then began to see her life—and the world—through these character strengths. She posted her character strengths profile in the kitchen, to serve as a catalyst for observing, discussing, remembering, and reflecting on character strengths. These top strengths were her lens for her interactions with others. She placed kindness and honesty at the forefront of each conversation with her husband—sharing her feelings and opinions about their communication over the years, but in a kind way. Although her job had been floundering, she brought a newfound lighthearted humor to her interaction with co-workers. She allowed curiosity to drive her search for new designs, to explore what worked and didn't work, and to question the opinions of her co-workers and customers. She looked for ways to be grateful for her capacity to design clothes and contribute to the joy of others. She saved the heaviest dosages of gratitude and humor for her two boys, whom she approached respectfully and slowly, and when the time was right offered playfulness and appreciation for their positive qualities and for their growing maturity and independence.

Each of these five strengths (and nineteen more) had always been there within Hannah. They had simply been numbed, lying dormant and underused as she went through the motions in life. It had never occurred to her to be more deliberate with her best qualities—to activate them in each of her interactions. Over the following weeks, her energy increased. She had purpose. Indeed, she had taken her life back. Months later, a casual observer could see Hannah's curious questioning, her verbal expressions of gratitude, her frequent laughter, her direct and honest approach in conversations, and her steady increase in thoughtful, caring actions for others.

Hannah had transformed her life. Two years later, Hannah's strengths profile remained in the same place in her kitchen, but now it was joined by her husband's and two sons' strengths profiles. The positive benefits for Hannah and her loved ones were clear: Hannah was maintaining her focus and enthusiasm for her own character strengths, was noticing and appreciating the character strengths of the people in her life, and was also inspiring others to ignite and appreciate their character strengths.

Why do character strengths matter? Let's examine this question from two perspectives, each of which occurred in Hannah's story. When things are going well, we can use character strengths to help us see what is best in ourselves and others. When things are going poorly, we can use character strengths to give balance to the struggles we face, to shift our focus from the negative to the positive, to avoid becoming overly self-critical by thinking about our strengths rather than what's wrong with us. Enacting the character strengths—our awe for beauty and excellence, or our curiosity—can help us notice the good things around us; discover how we can do better; and catalyze positive, virtuous, healthy, or more balanced behavior. Hold these important perspectives in your mind as we review them.

Amplifying and growing the positive: We can examine the importance of character strengths through a positive lens. Research has shown many positive benefits of using character strengths across physical, psychological, emotional, social, and spiritual domains. The benefits of character strengths have been demonstrated in many industries—especially business and education—but also in healthcare, coaching, and psychotherapy and counseling, to name a few. Specific benefits of character strengths have been linked with each of the main elements of well-being: positive emotions, engagement, meaning, positive relationships, and accomplishment. They've been connected with many other benefits that help us amplify the positive in our life, such as self-acceptance, autonomy, goal progress, physical health, passion, and resilience. The newest research is showing that techniques for helping people boost their strengths can have important advantages over techniques that focus on correcting their deficits. But focusing on the positive is not the same as ignoring the negative.

Learning from and reframing the negative: Research shows that humans demonstrate a number of biases in our thinking. One of those biases is the tendency to remember and be affected more by negative events than by positive events. Problems and upsetting emotions stick with us like glue. Strengths can help bring greater balance to this equation. We need negative experiences to learn from, motivate us, warn us, and help us grow. But those experiences should not define us. Reflecting on our strengths can help us offset those negative experiences, can help us figure out our natural best way to avoid them in the future, and can remind us that we have unique resources available to us in negative situations.

Nowhere does this negativity emerge more strongly than in the workplace. Research shows most of us are disengaged from the work we are doing. We go through the motions, get caught up in routines, and are not as productive as we could be. But research also suggests that when we make the most of our character strengths—and use them in our jobs—we become happier at work, more productive, and more engaged in what we are doing.

> Specific benefits of character strengths have been linked with each of the main elements of well-being

Research studies have also shown that the character strengths help us manage problems more effectively. For example, using character strengths has been linked with less stress and improved coping in the workplace, less friction in classrooms, less depression, and fewer physical symptoms, to name just a few settings in which character strengths have been studied.

Finally, all of us have blind spots in our self-understanding—there is no perfectly aware person. There's more that we don't know about ourselves than what we do know. And in some cases, others are more aware of how we are coming across than we are! As character strengths act like self-awareness boosters, they help us fill in some of these gaps in our self-knowledge.

A Shared Language

Imagine this: You walk into a room with a mixed group of people, and no one is able to communicate with anyone else—verbally or nonverbally. You wander from person to person, table to table, and are unable to connect. Each person speaks in a way that is foreign to you. You sense there is something there, some common ground, but you are unable to access it. There's a gap between you and every other person, and you have no tool to create a bridge. How would you feel: Confused? Frustrated? Disconnected? Left in the dark?

> Character strengths help us manage
> problems more effectively.

Before the mid-2000s, there was no "common language" for talking about what's best in people. There were books on virtues and positive qualities that individuals had written, but these were usually focused on the virtues of a specific religion or culture, particularly Western culture. It was at that point that the field of psychology really began to take on the question: What is best about human beings? The result, in 2004, was the VIA Classification of Character Strengths and Virtues. For the first time in history, we had a shared language for communicating with one another about our best selves. Now, as easily as speaking the same native tongue, we describe the bravery and perseverance of our co-worker, we reinforce the creativity and kindness of our child, we deliberately use our social intelligence when helping a person in need, and we tap into gratitude and hope for personal sustenance. This VIA Classification paved the way for hundreds of studies by scientists across the globe who are making new discoveries each month in advancing the science of character. This research, in turn, has catalyzed thousands of practitioners in psychology, coaching, education, business, and other fields to apply these new findings to bring out what's best in their clients, students, and employees.

Uniquely You

Character is plural. This is, according to the late scientist Christopher Peterson, the most important research finding in his more than fifteen years of study on character strengths and positive psychology. What Peterson meant by this is that character can't be captured in a single concept such as honesty or integrity. Rather, people express a variety of character strengths, and almost always are expressing multiple strengths at the same time.

Your character can be mapped out. It maps as a personal profile of strengths with highs and lows and mid-range character strengths. After you take the VIA Survey of strengths, one of several scientifically valid and free strengths tests offered by the VIA Institute on Character, you receive your profile of strengths from 1 to 24. This displays the rich tapestry of your character.

Interestingly, no one has the same profile of character strengths as you do. There are over 600 sextillion possible combinations (that is, the number 6 followed by 23 zeroes!) of the 24 character strengths, so profiles are rarely exactly the same.

The uniqueness does not end there. Although the 24 strengths exist in each of us, the way each person expresses each strength is unique. No one expresses those character strengths in the same way as you. Your personal strengths patterns reflect your unique humanity. Furthermore, in each situation of your life, you express your own combinations of character strengths, and that expression changes from situation to situation. In some situations, you will bring forth more zest (e.g., at a sporting event) or less zest (e.g., at a funeral home). In this way, your strengths are used in degrees of "more or less" rather than "good character or bad character" or "all or none." The "all or none" approach is standard for diagnosing medical problems or psychological disorders. If your blood sugar reaches a certain level over time, you are diagnosed with diabetes. If you meet certain criteria such as depressed mood, lack of motivation in pleasurable activities, and sleep/eating/concentration problems, then you have a depression diagnosis of some kind. These are "all or none" situations. In contrast, character strengths are a matter of degree. Your friend who asks lots of questions isn't "the curiosity person" and your mother isn't "the love person." There isn't a person who is the "good character" or "perfect character" person who uses all 24 strengths and makes no mistakes, just as there isn't a person who uses zero strengths and is completely "bad."

We are more complex—and versatile—than that. While curiosity and love might be very strongly expressed by certain individuals, they aren't *always* expressed by a particular person. There are times when they hold back their curiosity or love, and there are many times when they use other character strengths.

Nowhere is your uniqueness clearer than with your *signature strengths*. The concept of signature strengths is an important part of the VIA Classification. These are the strengths that are strongest or most prominent in your own strengths profile. With over 5.1 million possible combinations in your top five strengths, these are the elements of your character that warrant your closest attention. They hold great potential. Ultimately, they are likely to be the strengths that matter most to you, that are most central to your personal identity. At the VIA Institute, we find three key features are common in signature strengths, explained as "the 3 E's":

Essential	They feel essential to who you are as a person. The person for whom appreciation of beauty and excellence is a signature strength doesn't just like beauty: seeking out experiences of beauty is part of what makes them who they are.

Effortless	When you enact the strength, it feels natural and effortless. Being curious or kind isn't work; it just flows. Recent research suggests this sense of flow when using a character strength is the best single identifier of a signature strength.
Energizing	Using the strength energizes and uplifts you. It leaves you feeling happy, in balance, ready to take on more.

Research suggests that people who take the VIA Survey consider about five of the 24 strengths to be signature strengths on average. Explore these top strengths within yourself. Find new ways to express them at home, work, in relationships, and in your community. If you do, that is part of what is referred to as "being authentic."

In our work with the VIA Classification, we often say that all 24 character strengths matter. This means that all of the strengths have their benefits. This also means it doesn't matter which strengths are your personal signature strengths. What matters is that you know, explore, and use them, whatever they are. You might wish bravery was #1 and you lament that it comes in at #24. It's fine to boost it up, but a good recommendation is to first give substantial attention to noticing, exploring, appreciating, and expressing your top strengths.

After that, looking to how you bring forth your middle and lesser strengths and boosting those is an important approach to consider. Any of your middle or lesser strengths might actually serve as what we call a *phasic strength* in certain situations. A phasic strength is a non-signature strength that you bring forth strongly in a given situation. This occurs when you "rise to the occasion." For example, if you are low in bravery but acting as the lone voice sharing an unpopular opinion against a crowd of dissenters you might be using bravery as a phasic strength. If you are typically low in kindness but you see someone who is suffering on the street and you act swiftly and compassionately to help them with your time and money, you might be using kindness as a phasic strength.

Whether one of the 24 strengths is a signature strength, or a middle or lower strength that you may only use as a phasic strength, each strength can make a positive difference in your life and the lives of others. Remember, all the strengths matter.

Seeds to Nurture and Grow

Character strengths can be developed. The last decade of research in personality psychology has resulted in the exciting finding that our personality, including our character, can change. Your character tends to be consistent over time, but many factors can cause it to change. These can include changes in your life role, such as getting married, having a child, or joining the military; unexpected events, such as an experience of trauma (e.g., a natural disaster or experiencing abuse); and deliberate interventions you use to make a change.

Consider the metaphor of viewing your various character strengths as seeds.

Imagine this: you discover you have 24 seeds, each a different color and size. You plant them side by side, not knowing what will bloom. You make sure each seed gets sunlight, rich soil, and lots of water. You watch each seed carefully, noticing a few sprout quickly while others bud slowly. Over time, some grow into beautiful flowers, others into tall, leafy trees or hardy bushes. Others remain modest, just producing an unremarkable but hardy plant. Each is important to attend to, because what it becomes is a product not only of its internal makeup and the environment, but also of the attention you give it. And, each contributes its part to the local landscape.

Some of your character strengths may grow in an obvious way—flourishing and easily noticed by your friends and family. Other strengths can be overshadowed by your more dominant strengths, like a small flower attempting to grow underneath a leafy tree. You'll find that some of your character strengths have been dormant, unnoticed and unappreciated for months or even years. Other strengths are rough around the edges like a prickly rose bush. And some will appear weak like a plant drooping without water. In any case, for each of your character strengths, remember this adage: what you attend to grows. You can make an impact on these positive qualities.

> It is easy to take your strengths for granted

It is easy to take your strengths for granted. It is commonplace to overlook them. The reality is, though, that we use these strengths in many small ways that are important for our life. Many researchers have discussed how strengths can present as "Big" and "little." For example, "Big C" Creativity is something that has an enormous impact, such as Vincent van Gogh's *Starry Night*, while "little c" creativity is shown in your thinking of a new way to drive home that avoids bad traffic. Similarly, "Big L" Leadership can be seen in an influential and inspiring president or city mayor, while "small l" leadership is shown in your organizing an evening of fun for a group of four friends. As this book focuses more on the use of "little" character strengths, we offer an example for each of the 24 character strengths in the table that follows. By the way, don't interpret "little" as meaning insignificant or too small to be relevant; quite the contrary, we believe these uses of character strengths can build and amount to substantial benefits for yourself, for others, and for the larger community.

Character Strengths	Examples of "little" Uses
Wisdom Strengths	
Creativity	Trying a new clothes combination.
Curiosity	Looking up something online that interests you.
Judgment	Deciding someone is a bad influence and avoiding that person.
Love of Learning	Reading a long essay about a political or social issue.
Perspective	Remembering that some others have it worse than you when you're feeling overwhelmed.
Courage Strengths	
Bravery	Doing something that scares you, even a little.
Perseverance	Getting back to work on the task that does not interest you.
Honesty	Admitting when you have done something wrong.
Zest	Becoming excited about something in your day.
Humanity Strengths	
Love	Seeing and appreciating something positive in someone close to you that you have never noticed before.
Kindness	Complimenting a stranger on the street.
Social Intelligence	Realizing what someone is thinking before he or she even says it.

Character Strengths	Examples of "little" Uses
Justice Strengths	
Teamwork	Helping a colleague at work feel included on a project.
Fairness	Resolving a conflict with your partner in a way that both of you feel recognized.
Leadership	Outlining how to achieve a goal for a group.
Temperance Strengths	
Forgiveness	Letting a small insult go by without saying something mean in return.
Humility	Doing something good for someone without letting anyone know.
Prudence	Holding back when you are angry, instead of blowing up.
Self-Regulation	Exercising when you just do not feel like it.
Transcendence Strengths	
Appreciation of Beauty & Excellence	Noticing something new and beautiful in a painting or piece of music you have always liked.
Gratitude	Sincerely thanking someone for a small present.
Hope	Thinking about the positive outcome ahead during a stressful situation.
Humor	Making someone feel comfortable by telling a joke.
Spirituality	Reflecting on a sacred or highly meaningful moment you had with a loved one.

As your knowledge of and skills using these character strengths grows, your motivation to use them more in your life will also rise. It's not uncommon to see immediate points of impact for yourself and others. In order to keep the impact moving forward, it takes continued practice. This book provides you with the facts, examples, ideas, and practices to help you make and sustain positive impact. This is your resource for taking action to grow your strengths to new heights.

Getting Started

There are two great places to start when it comes to learning about and understanding your character strengths. One is to get comfortable and skilled with "strengths-spotting" in others. The other is to take the VIA Survey and familiarize yourself with your results. We'll focus on both here.

Strengths-spotting in others: "I feel so empowered!" said the young woman as she waved the list of 24 character strengths (the strengths profile you receive when you complete the VIA Survey) in the air. "I can see these strengths everywhere!" What this woman was observing is that once you have the language of 24 strengths in hand (or in head), you know what you are looking for. You understand the words and the full language of strengths, and you can be mindful of how they appear in many big and small ways in your life. People describe this experience with the 24 strengths as akin to their eyes opening wider and as new doors being opened inside them. With these positive qualities in mind, you can watch movies and television in a new way; you can take a fresh look at what people say on social media; you may notice strengths in characters of the books and magazines you are reading; and you can see strengths in every conversation in each of your relationships—with family, friends, co-workers, children, neighbors, and new people you encounter. There are strengths you can potentially appreciate everywhere you go.

We encourage you to begin strengths-spotting now!

Strengths-spotting involves two simple steps:

1. *During any observation or conversation, label the character strength you notice* (use the list and definitions of the 24 character strengths at the beginning of this book as a support). What is the positive quality you are observing? What character strength word best fits what you're seeing? For example, a character in a movie challenges herself to enter a dangerous situation, and you label this as bravery. The character of a young man is described in the book you're reading as jumping out of bed in the morning with a smile on his face, and you label this as zest.

2. *Describe how you see the character strength being expressed.* What is the behavior that is linked with the strength? What is your rationale for the strength you've chosen? What evidence supports your observation? For example, you observe your spouse engaging in an in-depth conversation with a neighbor, and you might say to them: "I noticed the good conversation you had with our neighbor. It seemed like you were using a lot of your curiosity because you were asking questions and exploring a variety of topics. I also noticed social intelligence in you because you seemed to empathize with some of the problems they were having and there was a good back and forth of sharing and listening in the conversation." Notice that you can spot multiple strengths in an interaction.

The example used for the second step also highlights the possibility of a third step. In many situations, especially those involving your close relationships, you might consider *strengths appreciation* as well. In this step, you affirm the value of the strength being expressed and convey that the person's strength expression matters to or benefits you or others. For this step, you can ask yourself, "Why does this person's character strength use matter to me, to others, or to them?"

We encourage you to begin strengths-spotting now! Keep the list of 24 character strengths and definitions handy. In the next conversation you have, the next TV show you watch, or the next tweet you read, what is the character strength being expressed by the person or by the character? What is your rationale for what you are observing? Taking this approach in the many facets of your daily life will help you build your skill of strengths-spotting, and deepen your understanding of the 24 character strengths and how they bring benefits to people's lives.

> All 24 of these character strengths matter, and they are all qualities within you that you can build

Take the VIA Survey: In addition to strengths-spotting, we suggest one more approach. Take the VIA Survey! It is the only free, online, well-tested test of these character strengths in the world. It is comprehensive, in that after you spend fifteen minutes taking it, you'll automatically receive your strengths profile, a personal rank-ordered list of the 24 strengths. Go to the VIA Institute website to take the test here: www.viacharacter.org. Print your free strengths profile to keep as a reference as you read this book.

As we have discussed, all 24 of these character strengths matter, and they are all qualities within you that you can build. It is interesting to look at your whole profile and understand (and potentially boost) your middle or lower strengths, but again, we suggest the best thing you can do at this point is to give the closest attention to your highest strengths, your signature strengths.

We say this because these are likely to be the closest descriptors of "the real you," the easiest for you to broaden, and the ones that serve as an immediate resource for good times and bad. In addition, there is good research support for the advantages of using your signature strengths more in your life.

We suggest keeping your signature strengths handy as you go through this book. Many people will decide to go directly to their signature strengths in Part II to deepen their awareness and exploration of their best qualities (and then explore their signature strengths more closely in Part III). We have provided space below for you to jot down your signature strengths. Research by the VIA Institute has found that people generally have about five signature strengths. That is a general starting point for considering your top strengths, but feel free to plug in more as you come to understand the most essential, most energizing, and most effortless parts of you.

Signature strength #1: _____

Signature strength #2: _____

Signature strength #3: _____

Signature strength #4: _____

Signature strength #5: _____

Now that you've begun to familiarize yourself with your signature strengths and strengths-spotting in others, let's move on to Part II and take a closer look at each of the 24 character strengths. Each one is a part of your personality that is packed with positive energy and potential benefits for you and the important people in your life!

PART II:

EXPLORING THE 24 CHARACTER STRENGTHS

Your Guide to the 24 Character Strengths

The structure of What-Why-How is applied to each of the 24 character strengths. You can expect the following for these sections:

What to Know About the Strength

In this section, you will learn the basics about each character strength, including its basic elements and meanings.

Use these sections on "the what" to get a general working understanding about the strength, its many pieces and parts, and how it can play out when you are at your best.

Why the Strength Is Valuable

In this section, you will learn what science has shown about each character strength. We'll deal with questions like:

- Why does this particular character strength matter?
- Why use this strength?

- What outcomes might be expected if you regularly use this strength in a balanced way in your life?

Use these sections on "the why" to better understand the power and substance behind each strength. As you learn the many unique benefits of each strength, you will appreciate the strength in a deeper way, especially knowing that you have that strength within you.

How to Ignite the Strength

There are four parts to this section to offer you a variety of paths for bringing each character strength to the forefront of your life. These four parts offer you activities you can do alone or with others.

REFLECTING

Self-reflection and self-exploration are important for building insights into one's character. For each strength, you'll find a number of questions you can think about, journal on, or discuss with others. This kind of reflection helps us draw connections between new ideas about the strengths and past experiences. The more time you spend reflecting on these questions and discussing them with others, the more likely you'll experience emotional "Aha!" insights about you and your strengths. These insights can be the beginnings of important personal growth in your life.

Use these Reflecting sections to explore the unexpected depths that each strength has to offer. We suggest pausing, even for a few seconds, after each question to allow your mind to remember, to mull over, and to imagine.

SPOTTING THE STRENGTH

Research indicates that one of the most powerful ways to enable or boost a character strength is to learn by observing others. This might come in the form of role models, mentors, or hearing and connecting with people's stories of strengths use. Your observation of others has played a crucial role in your learning since you were a young child. When we observe the behaviors of others, our brains take in that information and file it away as a guide for our future use when we are in a situation where we might need it. If you are around a lot of creative people at work, you quickly learn a range of new ways to think about things, to solve problems, and to come up with new ideas. If you are around many kind people in your family, you will have that information (i.e., various ways to be kind, generous, thoughtful, compassionate, caring) filed away. Someday you may copy one or more of those behaviors in your life or do something very similar. Of course, you might not, as there is no guarantee that you will learn what you have observed or that you will carry out similar behaviors.

This section, Spotting the Strength, takes advantage of the benefits of our learning from others by offering a compelling, everyday example of a person using a particular strength. (We have taken necessary steps to protect the identity of the actual person). These stories target the use of one strength in each example, but it goes without saying that each of these individuals used many other character strengths, some equally as strong as the one being focused on. Remember, character is plural: each of us has many strengths and we are using many of them at once rather than one at a time in isolation. Here, we go beyond behavior, to reflect how role models shape your character identity.

Use these Spotting the Strength sections to make use of the wisdom of others. Read the example, which is offered in the person's own words, sharing their story of the character strength's impact on their life. See the uniqueness of the person's character and consider how you express that character strength in your life.

TAKING ACTION

Sometimes the best recipe for action is to have something tangible placed in front of you. Therefore, seven to ten concrete, practical strategies are offered as ideas for using each character strength in daily life. Some of these are evidence- or research-based activities and others are commonsense wisdom. The strategies are offered with consideration of common domains of life that people participate in: relationships, work, and community. A fourth category is offered for each character strength—that of turning the character strength inward, applying it to yourself. Hundreds of studies show the benefit of character strengths across a wide range of people—no matter what their age, profession, or gender—in a wide range of life domains, including work, school, social life, and close relationships. In addition, research is emerging around the importance of taking a character strength that is typically expressed outwardly such as kindness, forgiveness, or perspective/wisdom and turning it inward. In this way, for example, the strength of kindness becomes self-compassion, and forgiveness becomes self-forgiveness. These approaches have shown a range of well-being benefits.

Use these Taking Action sections to move from strength awareness and strength exploration into strength application! Choose one strategy to start with. Consider whether you might do the activity with someone or by yourself. After you take action, monitor your experiences and the experiences of others.

FINDING BALANCE

When you express your character strengths in your actions, that is not a guarantee that what you do will be successful, well-received by others, or the best choice for the situation. You can overuse a strength by coming across too intensely for the situation or by negatively impacting another person unintentionally. You are even more vulnerable to regularly underusing your strengths, such as by not putting your best foot forward, not challenging yourself, not paying attention, or not being authentic. You can come across as uninterested or lacking in empathy or care for others. Learning to become mindful of such underuse or overuse will help you go a long way toward improving your character strengths use and creating positive outcomes for yourself and others. As strengths overuse can be particularly tricky to understand, we offer an everyday example of a person describing how they fell into the trap of strengths overuse.

In addition to describing how overuse and underuse might play out with each character strength, we suggest an additional way to find balance with character strengths use, a way that has for thousands of years been called "the golden mean" or "the middle way": to consider what *optimal use*, the sweet spot between overuse and underuse, might look like for each character strength. For this, we offer a one-sentence motto for optimal use of each strength, inspired by research on the overuse, underuse, and optimal use of each character strength. This is followed by an "imagine this" activity that explores the optimal use of the strength in general or in a particular situation. In most cases, this activity includes additional character strengths, usually those that are especially complementary to the strength being focused on (i.e., strengths found in research studies to highly correlate with the strength that's being focused on). There is no exact way to make sure you use the perfect amount of a character strength, or avoid its underuse or overuse. There are only concepts, ideas, examples, and ways of thinking about our lives through these lenses. With a thoughtful approach, you can become more comfortable, confident, and competent with your character strengths use.

Use these Finding Balance sections to move into more advanced character strengths work. Start by spotting your strengths overuse and underuse. Understand how there are many ways each strength can be expressed too strongly or too weakly. Some of these will be very subtle, and you can improve your strength use as you attend to them. Others will be much broader overuses or underuses that you discover negatively affect you or others. Be sure to be not only honest but kind with yourself as you explore these imbalances.

Remember that this is a learning exercise about getting to know yourself better so treat these insights as useful information, rather than an opportunity to beat yourself up. Objective self-review is an important part of optimal strengths use!

Next, consider for yourself what optimal use might look like in a particular situation. This may change quite a bit based on where we are and who we are with! Use the "imagine this" scenario to consider how that strength might look when expressed in a balanced way, and how it might be expressed with other character strengths.

THE 24 VIA CHARACTER STRENGTHS

VIRTUE OF WISDOM

CREATIVITY   CURIOSITY   JUDGMENT   LOVE OF LEARNING   PERSPECTIVE

Strengths That Help You Gather and Use Knowledge

In the VIA Classification, the virtue of wisdom has to do with gaining knowledge and using that knowledge effectively to solve problems. Wisdom is related to intelligence, but it is different. A person can be naturally smart, but that does not mean they put effort into learning deeply about the world, challenging their beliefs to make sure they are correct, and being open-minded to the possibility they are wrong. In fact, people who are very smart can sometimes become invested in always being right or smarter than everyone else. As a result, they can miss opportunities to learn from their own mistakes or correct their misconceptions. The person who is marked by wisdom is eager to learn about the world, even at the risk of having to accept being wrong. This eagerness to some extent reflects a basic desire to learn. The person high in wisdom learns about a variety of topics that influence his or her ability to act in the world. Wisdom also presents itself in a desire to understand the world with the goal of operating more effectively in that world.

A particularly important aspect of wisdom is what has been called "practical wisdom." This is an ancient concept, one that comes to us from the classical Greeks. This is the ability to figure out the ends you want to achieve and the best way to achieve those ends. For this reason, wisdom is important to knowing how to use the other strengths effectively to achieve your goals. It is also important to knowing how to use your strengths to achieve good in the world. The strengths that are considered pathways to the virtue of wisdom include *creativity*, *curiosity*, *judgment*, *love of learning*, and *perspective*.

CREATIVITY

WHAT	WHY	HOW

What to Know About Creativity

Creativity is thinking of new ways to do things. It involves producing ideas or behaviors that are original. However, originality is not enough: whatever is created, whether an idea or a product, must also be useful or adaptable. For example, you might write a blog post that is unique because it is entirely gibberish. That's likely not going to be useful, so would not be considered creative.

Like all character strengths, creativity is found in degrees. At one end of the spectrum are those individuals who are widely recognized for their exceptional creativity, such as great scientists, poets, filmmakers, and painters. This is often referred to as "Big C" creativity. "Small c" creativity is everyday creativity and ingenuity: when you come up with a new, more direct route home or you think of a new way to solve a problem. Most people are capable of everyday, "small c" creativity. What really distinguishes a creative person is not intelligence; it is their general tendency to approach new dilemmas with a commitment to trying new solutions.

If you demonstrate strong creativity, then you can generate unique ideas and strategies that build your knowledge and the knowledge of others. You probably find that people gravitate toward you when they are looking for feedback on their own creative projects, or are looking for help solving problems that are stumping them. When you're at your best with creativity, you make connections and put ideas together in unique ways that inspire others and lead to new and interesting ideas.

WHAT **WHY** **HOW**

Why Creativity Is Valuable

Research findings on the benefits of the strength of creativity include the following:

- Creativity helps in promoting divergent thinking, thinking about many ways to solve a problem. It uses ideas and details in a way that can be implemented for a socially positive purpose.
- Creativity helps you resolve practical problems, especially when you begin thinking in new ways about the causes and consequences of everyday life events.
- Self-confidence and greater self-knowledge are byproducts of creativity that can help you feel comfortable in a variety of situations and adapt to challenges and stressors.
- Creativity helps to inspire and motivate followers and can help you become a better leader.
- Creativity drives your interest in activities and can help you generate ideas that will inspire interest in others.

- The tendency to be creative is fairly stable over time, but it can be enhanced by settings that are supportive, reinforcing, open, and informal. On the other hand, creativity can be impeded by time pressures, close supervision by others, or critical examination by yourself or others.

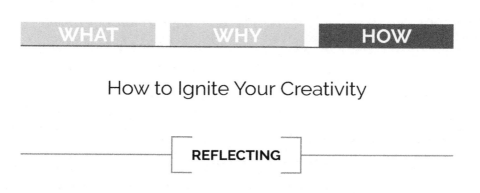

How to Ignite Your Creativity

REFLECTING

Consider these questions as you reflect on your strength of creativity:

- What encourages your creativity?
- What holds you back from trying to be creative?
- How do real or anticipated reactions of other people affect your creative efforts?
- What does creativity mean to you and how does that definition play out in your life?
- How do you use creativity to help solve your own life problems or those of your family, friends, and colleagues?

SPOTTING THE STRENGTH

Meet Juanita L., an artist who specializes in puppet shows for children:

I love to create—without creativity in my life, I feel like the world would be in black and white. The way I use my creativity is I just "go for it" each day. I find unique ways to express myself. What I create doesn't have to be beautiful. For example, I read a thing about how to turn old T-shirts into yarn. One day, I turned my shirts into potholders and a rug for outside my mud room. The next day I would experiment with cooking and combine ingredients I already had in my house. The day after that, I started decorating a new wall in my living room.

I regularly throw myself into these sorts of artsy projects with abandon. It's a way that I wake up a part of myself, and it keeps me going in a positive direction.

As a kid, I loved watching Sesame Street. *I had three puppets I would practice with in my room. I would spend hours singing songs with them, having dialogues with them, and making up problems they could solve together. When inanimate things come to life, it is one of my favorite things, and when I see it in the faces of thousands of children when that thing comes to life, it's amazing.*

Looking back, creativity has always played a central role in my life. I was adopted, in a family where discussing my adoption was discouraged. As the "good child," I turned to invention to protect myself from feeling isolated. My creativity popped out, and I guess that's how I dealt with my feelings of not fitting in or not being at home. Creativity is how I learned to cope.

As an adult, I don't make time to create new things every day, but I still use my creativity in other ways. I'm good at coming up with lots of ways to solve problems. My son will come home from school with a difficulty with his math homework or a conflict with a bully at school, and I'll immediately have four or five ways he can solve the problem. Sometimes we discuss each idea and other times I try to come up with the best one for him.

TAKING ACTION

In relationships

- Explore a creative solution to a life difficulty or challenge that's expressed by a family member or a friend.
- Examine an event from your past with your family or an intimate relationship in which creativity was used for the benefit of everyone involved.

At work

- At your next work meeting, when a new topic comes up, brainstorm several ideas with the group to reflect on or discuss together.
- With one of your typical work tasks, think of a new and unique way to complete it. Do it at least two times this week in that new way.
- Prioritize creativity at work. Set aside a few minutes each day for "creativity time" where you can reflect, think, and learn.

Within your community

- Write an article, essay, short story, or poem, make a drawing or painting, and share it with others.

Turned inward

- Take a problem you are facing. Deliberately develop multiple solutions for the problem rather than just one.

FINDING BALANCE

Underuse of creativity

There will be situations that call for creativity where you will suppress it. This is most likely in situations where people are closed off, rigid, authoritarian, or overly critical. You might find that time pressure can also inhibit your creativity, especially if you are someone who values having plenty of time for an idea to incubate. In other words, you find that reflection time is important for you to generate creative ideas that will help you "connect the dots." If you don't share this need with others, you might be perceived by them as underusing your creativity. In other situations, you might have a very useful and creative idea, but personal barriers get in the way, such as self-doubts, doubts about the value of your idea, feeling nervous about sharing, feeling concerned you might offend someone, or feeling a lack of confidence about your idea. You may also have concerns that if you share a new way to do something, it might implicitly be sending a message to others that their ideas are not good enough.

To underuse your creativity deliberately is to be a conformist in a particular situation. At times, this is entirely appropriate and wise, while at other times it's blocking who you are, and may even result in a solution that doesn't feel right.

Overuse of creativity

The overuse of creativity might immediately call to mind the wild-haired thinker with crazy ideas he or she thinks will change the world but that everyone else knows are pointless. This image may be extreme, but it makes the point. Too much thinking in new ways, in ways that don't ever pay off, doesn't serve anyone well.

While your creativity can energize you, it can also be overwhelming to others, as the number of ideas, changes, or projects may be "too much" for a particular situation. This can be a source of tension for both you and those working or living with you. Also, if you are high in creativity but low in perseverance, you may struggle to complete projects and leave a lot of loose ends or new initiatives unfinished. You can also end up feeling irritated by others who don't show appreciation for your innovation and new ways of doing things. A useful question to ask yourself is whether others resonate with your creative ideas.

Jim S., a marketing executive, tells his story of overusing creativity:

When I went to college, I was free to pursue whatever I wanted for the very first time in my life. I was learning and seeing all these new ways to do things. I had the freedom to create! There were many options, so many possible outlets for all my ideas. I started lots of projects because I felt there were many things to experiment with. I got so engrossed in following up on my new ideas, I stopped going to classes that felt boring to me. Things did not turn out very well academically for me.

In the end, I was disappointed with how I'd done in college. I think my teachers ended up thinking of me as kind of a flake, so I wasn't able to rely on them for recommendations for jobs. I knew I could have done much better. I had been excited by all the projects I was taking on at the time, imagining all sorts of potential with each one, but there were so many that I didn't make the time to see any of them through in a thorough way.

Optimal use of creativity:
The golden mean

Creativity motto:

"I am creative, conceptualizing something useful, coming up with ideas that result in something worthwhile."

Imagine this:

Imagine you are a particularly creative team member. You create new products and come up with new ideas that are beneficial to others. You find balance by contributing strongly at team brainstorming meetings, building on others' ideas and offering new avenues of thought. At the same time, though, you monitor your team members' facial expressions and feedback so that you don't "take over" the meeting. At another meeting later that day, you take a backseat as it's a business meeting with less room or time for brainstorming, but you do speak up to explain one idea that would help with a project. In these situations, you are using your creativity along with perspective (seeing the bigger picture) and social intelligence (monitoring the reactions of others).

CURIOSITY

What to Know About Curiosity

To be curious is to explore and discover, to take an interest in ongoing experience for its own sake. Curiosity is often described as novelty-seeking and being open to experience, and it's associated with the natural desire to build knowledge. It is fulfilling to journey toward an answer, to engage in a new experience, or to learn a new fact. To go to a new restaurant, visit a new city, meet a new person in your class, or to conduct an online search for a question can each fulfill your quest for new experiences and new information.

If you are particularly curious, you have a desire to pursue the new and the different, and at times, to explore the complex, the uncertain, and the ambiguous. Being open to new experiences is like a trademark for you and is a likely contributor to your personal growth. Your curiosity leads you to take an active interest in ongoing life experiences where you may be ready to explore virtually anything—new people, places, situations, and work. When you are at your best with curiosity, your mind is on fire with wonder and interest. You actively seek information and ask questions that satisfy your driving curiosity while exercising the good judgment to control your questioning when it causes discomfort for others.

WHAT   WHY   HOW

Why Curiosity Is Valuable

Research findings on the benefits of the strength of curiosity include the following:

- Curiosity is one of the five strengths most reliably linked to satisfaction with life.
- Curiosity is associated with happiness, health and longevity, and positive social relationships.
- Curiosity can strengthen a marital relationship by keeping it new and interesting.
- Curiosity helps in seeking and finding greater meaning in life.
- Curiosity helps in embracing uncertain and new situations.
- Curiosity is often the entry point to many lifelong hobbies, passions, and pursuits.
- Curious people are more attracted to activities that offer opportunities for growth, competence, and a higher level of stimulation. Thus, they are likely to report having personal goals aimed at self-improvement, such as wanting to know more about their character strengths!

CURIOSITY

How to Ignite Your Curiosity

REFLECTING

Consider these questions as you reflect on your strength of curiosity:

- What are you most curious about?
- With which people or in what circumstances do you feel most comfortable or encouraged in expressing curiosity?
- Were you a curious child and adolescent? How has your curiosity been affected growing up? If it has changed over time, why is that?
- When you start to wonder about something, what gets in the way of your moving that curiosity into action? What helps you make the most of your curiosity?
- How does curiosity play out across the different domains of your life—family, socializing, work, school?

SPOTTING THE STRENGTH

Meet Georgio C., 28, an information technology professional:

My feeling is that the mental stimulation of asking questions and being curious opens the channels to do the thinking I need to do. Even when I was young, I was always asking questions.

I became really curious about computers when I was a teenager. Other kids would just play on their computers and not think about what was going on under the hood, but I was really curious. I opened it up, looked inside, wondered what everything did. I started reading about it, and asking questions. I drove people nuts with my questions. But that's what I do—when I meet somebody new, it's never a problem for me. I know I can always ask them one, two, or ten questions. There's always something that piques my interest. Every social interaction is an opportunity that may never be repeated. In every situation, you could have a gem.

I'm curious about animals, plants, minerals, planes, sports, pottery, meditation, and so on. Food and travel, though, are probably my favorites. Both teach me so much about people, other cultures, customs, and social interactions. They say you can never travel to the same place twice—that fits me and how I'm always seeing new places with fresh eyes. And don't get me started on food! There are an infinite number of food combinations and choices; sometimes I think my taste buds are the most curious part of me! I work in an office full of guys. You could walk in with a broken arm—I'd have a thousand questions and nobody else would say anything. I've been stumped why so many people are uninterested in other people's lives.

TAKING ACTION

In relationships

- Bring curiosity to your relationships by trying to understand what people are thinking and feeling. Ask them direct questions, such as, "How are you feeling?" and "What are your thoughts about that?" Be curious about how others have approached challenges similar to those you are facing.

- Make a list of unknowns about one of the people with whom you feel very close. When you're ready, ask them a question or two. Invite them to ask you questions in return.

- Ask someone close to you what they are curious about and find ways to explore the topic together.

At work

- Try asking "why?" more often on your team or with your subordinates and supervisors to express more curiosity at work. Don't take what you're told at face value if it doesn't make complete sense to you.

- Practice being curious about a work activity that you dislike doing or have lost interest in. When performing the activity you dislike, look for at least three novel or unique features of this activity while you do it.

- Approach co-workers you don't know as well as others. Ask them one or two questions about their work, how their week is going, or their personal lives.

Within your community

- Try a new food today or go to a new restaurant to explore different foods and places.

- Drive a different route home to explore a new area near where you live.

- Do an online search for community activities going on around you. Take notice of what piques your curiosity most.

Turned inward

- Be curious about yourself. Take an interest in reflecting on your values, your hopes for the future, and the positive you have brought into the world through family, work, and community. Try to learn something new about the motivations you have for doing the things you do. Take action driven by your curiosity that aligns with what matters most to you.

FINDING BALANCE

Underuse of curiosity

When you use too little curiosity in a situation, you can appear to others as bored, uninterested, tired, distracted, or self-involved. These are commonplace behaviors, so they tell us quite a bit about the natural rise and fall of curiosity in a typical day. Cues such as glazed-over eyes, looking away, passive body language, and distractibility are quickly sized up by people. You may decide that underusing curiosity is the right choice for you in that situation, but it can be important to monitor how you might be coming across.

It's also important to make sure you're not suppressing your curiosity in a situation where it might actually turn out to be helpful to you and to others. Some people dampen their curiosity in situations where there is a strong authority figure in charge or where they feel anxious, or in situations where it's expected to follow directions instead of asking questions.

When you feel disengaged from a conversation, project, routine, or task, you might be on autopilot, simply going through the motions of life, not paying attention to the details and nuances around you. You might decide to allow yourself to stay there, but you might also want to consider using curiosity to pull yourself out of it.

Overuse of curiosity

When you don't keep your curiosity in check, you can offend others by being nosy or intrusive. It's natural to want to know what's going on in others' lives, to be curious about their secrets and their struggles, but expressing too much curiosity can make them uncomfortable and want to withdraw from you. Very curious people can be perceived by some as overly excited, or as rude or impolite.

You also might notice yourself getting distracted from the task at hand. The Internet can be particularly dangerous for the overly curious, who can find themselves searching for answers to whatever questions cross their minds instead of getting work done. When you're dealing with something uncomfortable or unpleasant, using your curiosity to help you cope with it can be a good thing. The saying "curiosity killed the cat" points to the dangers inherent in curiosity overuse.

Meet Jade S., 33, an event planner, shares about her curiosity overuse:

All my life people have called me nosey. I've gotten used to it. I've accepted it. I even wear it like a sort of brand or trademark. It's who I am. I'm highly curious. And I love people, so I start asking them questions. When they give me a little, my mind starts going a mile a second and I try to take more and more. I ask them about their work life, their personal life, their relationships, their pets, their interests, their travels. Some people really like it, and we connect. But many people get turned off quickly and pull away, or make an excuse to end the conversation. Occasionally, I get people telling me to mind my own business.

It has led me to get new customers and to keep them returning. But I've lost customers too. My supervisor has talked to me about this—to not fire so many questions at people. I try to manage it a bit, slow my mind down, take a breath. But other times I just let it all out with reckless abandon! Fire away!

Optimal use of curiosity:
The golden mean

Curiosity motto:

"I seek out situations where I gain new experiences without getting in my own or other people's way."

Imagine this:

Imagine you are curious about the life of someone you are talking with. You have just met the person for the first time and are intrigued by them, by their story. You are interested in knowing what they think, feel, and have done. You ask them questions, and you give them time to share responses and stories about each one. You offer similar sharing on your behalf as well in order to keep some balance in the conversation.

You realize that while questions are part of the ingredients of connecting more, not all questions are appropriate in this situation. As you talk with them, some thoughts pop up that seem a bit random and out of place. Out of curiosity, you share one or two of these to gather the person's opinion and impression on the topics.

As the conversation continues to be engaging, you realize you can keep it going with additional exploring and sharing. With other people, you might pause, change the topic, or explain that you'd like to talk more sometime. In this situation, you use your curiosity, along with other strengths, to keep the engagement level high. You see the elevations in your creativity as you come up with new topics to explore with the person and love of learning to dig deeper into each area. You notice your enthusiasm (zest) and positive feelings about a future connection with this person (hope) increase as well. Your strengths of perspective and prudence offer a balance to your curiosity as they help you see the big picture around building new connections: that it takes time and, to some degree, caution and reflection.

JUDGMENT/ CRITICAL THINKING

| **WHAT** | WHY | HOW |

What to Know About Judgment/Critical Thinking

Judgment involves making rational and logical choices, and analytically evaluating ideas, opinions, and facts. To use a term that originally came from outside the character field: it is critical thinking, weighing the evidence fairly, thinking things through, and examining the evidence from all sides rather than jumping to conclusions. Judgment also involves being open-minded and able to change one's mind in the light of evidence, remaining open to other arguments and perspectives. It should be clear at this point that judgment is a core "strength of the head"—it's a very thinking-oriented character strength.

Cognitive psychology has begun to reveal some important truths about how people make decisions. In reality, people rarely have the time or inclination to ferret out every potentially relevant piece of information or consider every possible view when making a decision. Instead, they quickly identify the key pieces of information and weigh those. It is this process of identifying the critical details, and thinking about them clearly and fairly, that is the hallmark of the person with good judgment.

That said, compared to other people, the person with good judgment also considers more options, to the point that he or she can feel as if they are taking a 360° view of the problem, situation, or idea. This practice helps to see things clearly and to avoid common thinking traps, such as catastrophizing (i.e., thinking that a small problem is a big one), when things go wrong. The person with good judgment also tries to avoid the common tendency to think in ways that favor their current views and to look for information that is consistent with those views. For example, someone high in this strength would not espouse one strong political view and then stick with news sources that unilaterally support that view. Rather, those using this strength would seek out multiple sources and views.

Judgment can help you make decisions and be someone who evaluates different sides of an issue fairly, with no or limited bias, without jumping to conclusions. When you are at your best using judgment/critical thinking, you weigh the issues, try to be objective in balancing the options, and are flexible in that your mind can be changed in light of new, solidly grounded evidence.

WHAT	WHY	HOW

Why Judgment/Critical Thinking Is Valuable

Research findings on the benefits of the strength of judgment/critical thinking include the following:

- People who can see things from more than one perspective are particularly skilled in dealing with times of change and transition.
- Judgment counteracts biased thinking, contributing to more accurate decision-making.
- Open-mindedness, a result of good judgment, contributes to the search for meaning in life by helping one to develop a broader understanding of how people find deeper meaning and purpose in their life.
- Individuals with this strength are less swayed by singular events and are more resistant to suggestion and manipulation.

WHAT   **WHY**   **HOW**

How to Ignite Your Judgment/Critical Thinking

REFLECTING

Consider these questions as you reflect on your strength of judgment/critical thinking:

- How do you express your judgment/critical thinking to others?
- When do you find that emotions get in the way of your ability to be objective? When is that most likely to occur for you?
- What people and circumstances bring out your analytic side? What brings you to your emotional or intuitive side?
- When you are trying to make decisions, what leads you to lose perspective of the big picture?

- How do you integrate your emotions or the emotions of others into a rational thinking process?
- With what people and in what circumstances is it difficult for you to think rationally without being confused by strong emotions?

SPOTTING THE STRENGTH

Meet Jackie B., 54, a university professor in communications:

I think it was natural for me to pursue a career that had something to do with political opinion. It's my job to listen to what other people say and decide whether it's accurate, whether it rings true. I consider it a central skill in the modern world, because people use emotional language so much of the time to try to get their way. I try very hard to teach my students to be critical of the things they read and hear.

It's not just in my job, though. I've always been someone who thought a long time about things I read or heard, and asked myself how much of what I'm hearing is based in logic and facts and how much is based in opinion or emotion. I try to understand the logic of what people are saying and see if it really makes sense. I was raised in a religious family, and my family used to give me a hard time about being skeptical about what I heard in church. They thought I never believed anything, but that's not true. I just wanted to evaluate what was being said and judge for myself whether it passed muster or not.

Here's a good example. Before I see a doctor, I seek out reputable sources of healthcare information on the Internet. They will often be

much more cautious about the value of a test than my doctor will be.
I go to my doctor armed with information that I've read, and nine
times out of ten, they'll agree it makes more sense to wait and see. It's
made me a much better caretaker for my own and my family's health.

TAKING ACTION

In relationships

- Go out of your way to discuss topics that are important to you with people whose opinions differ from yours. Evaluate the information and consider whether you might adjust your opinion.
- As you gather information about a person, weigh it based on its merits, and analyze the information rationally so you can keep any tendency to jump to conclusions in check.
- When a person expresses an opinion very different from your own, tell them what you believe and explore the basis for the difference with them. Ask them one or two clarifying questions about their opinion or approach.

At work

- When you make decisions based on a critical analysis of the problem, you are exercising good judgment. Consider a current work project. Express judgment by adding another angle or opinion to the project, maybe something new or an option that you may have rejected too quickly at first.
- Choose one of your work tasks where there is some disagreement about how to get it done. Use your critical thinking to examine the case for each view on the best solution.

- If you feel you might be biased about a particular problem at work, take an investigative approach and examine all the opposing views clearly and constructively.
- Those high in judgment love to get into the small details of projects, conversations, and work tasks, and to look at issues and problems from multiple angles and viewpoints. Think of a situation when this capacity was helpful to your boss or team. Appreciate your use of judgment in that situation.

Within your community

- Choose a strong opinion you have and live briefly (in a positive way) as if you have the opposite opinion. If acting as if you hold that opinion is too challenging, then experiment with this as a mental activity.
- Watch a political program that shares a very different or opposite point of view from your own, and try to understand how others could believe that position deeply.
- Read an online article from a spiritual, religious, atheist, etc. blogger who is sharing beliefs different from your own. Practice keeping an open mind that lets go of prejudging.

Turned inward

- The judgment strength helps you find holes in what people are saying or how they are acting. In this case, use your judgment to evaluate yourself and think critically about one of your personality qualities. Consider the pros and cons of this quality, and how it impacts you positively and negatively. Be sure to look for the "holes" - those areas you were not previously seeing, acknowledging, or accepting about this quality within you.

┌──────────────────────────┐
FINDING BALANCE
└──────────────────────────┘

Underuse of judgment/critical thinking

In some situations, when you bring too little of your critical thinking, you might appear as unreflective and not having much to offer the conversation. In other situations, an underuse of critical thinking might mean you are getting overly caught up in emotion or passion, and not listening adequately to other opinions. At these times, your hot emotions are interfering with cool thinking, and you need to turn down the temperature. In this situation, some people defend their hot-headed approach on the grounds that their position is right and no amount of argument should shake that belief. Consider this alternative: if your position is right, then rational argument should support that conclusion. If those expressing an alternative position start arguing emotionally, you can point that out but still try to see the logic in their argument. If you start arguing emotionally, then you're not really trusting the evidence for your opinion.

Underuse of judgment can be particularly dangerous in a conflict situation. It can lead you to say things that in retrospect are embarrassing and regrettable. In a situation where it is easy to become highly emotional, analyzing the situation and what that person is saying or doing, perhaps even confronting them on their behavior, can help defuse the tension.

Sometimes critical thinking is squashed by parents, authority figures, and others. It's common to see critical thinking discouraged in society, in politics, in religion, and even in many private institutions and schools.

While most people want to find support and agreement with their beliefs and opinions, it is narrow-minded to view those who are different as wrong. This is an underuse of judgment/critical thinking.

The expression of critical thinking can sometimes be discouraged in certain intimate relationships. For example, parents may have a difficult time with their adult children who begin to share alternative views. Another example is a relationship partner who acts as an authoritarian and refuses to accept the differing opinions of their relationship partner.

Overuse of judgment/critical thinking

It's easy to think of the overuse of judgment—it's being judgmental of yourself or of others. Most people relate to having experiences in which they judged and criticized themselves too harshly. While it's normal to have a judging part of your mind that motivates you and thinks things through, it's less beneficial to be chronically mean and negative about your daily actions and missteps.

This emphasis on the negative or imbalance toward criticism can carry over to your actual dialogue in your relationships. You might find that you are quick to judge new people you meet or those people who are closest to you. The challenge is to offer constructive feedback to others that offers honest pros and cons, positives and negatives, and suggestions for improvement. Many teachers, employers, parents, and supervisors veer far too much to the negative, where the feedback includes not much more than a token positive comment offered here or there. This can become an entrenched habit, one in which the individual has no idea this has become his or her style of critical thinking.

Friends and intimate partners often want you to support their ideas or simply validate their emotions, not judge them rationally.

It's important to make sure that those close to you feel heard and validated. Too much evaluation of others' opinions can leave them feeling disconnected from you. In these situations, judgment should be accompanied by a heavy dose of listening, kindness, social intelligence, and self-regulation. The use of curiosity can also help in exploring the other person's opinions and ideas.

Too much judgment can also take on the form of indecisiveness in an endless quest for all the necessary information and points of view to make a good decision. People who rely too heavily on judgment can therefore miss opportunities, because their strength becomes an obstacle to moving forward when decisions have to be made. Remember, good decision-making often doesn't involve knowing everything there is to know. The truth is that most decisions must be made with a limited amount of information. A highly reasoned approach can become overly rational at times, not giving enough consideration to emotions. This can be particularly frustrating when you are interacting with others who make more intuitive or emotional decisions.

Dave R., a 54-year-old banker, had this to say about the overuse of judgment:

> *I think being someone who doesn't take things at face value, who doesn't just accept things as true because they sound good, those are good things. They keep me from jumping to conclusions. But it can make me seem cynical. People sometimes think of me as really negative, but it's just that I'm being critical about what I'm hearing. But there are times when even I think I'm being a bit of a downer. I've had to learn at social events that when people are saying something as if it's the truth, and I know there's another side to it, I don't need to point that out.*

JUDGMENT/CRITICAL THINKING

My relationship with my wife has probably suffered the most from my critical thinking. Sometimes she brings up an idea that she just means to introduce casually, and I get all intense about evaluating it. One time she said to me, "Can I tell you I'm thinking about going to the supermarket without having to hear all the pros and cons?" We laughed about it, and I got it, and I've been trying to be more casual about decisions that aren't that important, or opinions that rub me the wrong way.

Optimal use of judgment/critical thinking:
The golden mean

Judgment/critical thinking motto:

"I weigh all aspects objectively in making decisions, including arguments that are in conflict with my convictions."

Imagine this:

Imagine you are approaching situations with a balance of both the head and the heart, a combination of slow, methodical, rational thinking while also considering quicker intuitive thinking and personal feelings. Notice that your approach at home with critical thinking is different from when you are with friends in the community, and different again from when you're at work. You can see that somewhere in this balance lies wisdom.

When you start to get hung up in the details, you can use perspective to refocus on the big picture, the need for a decision, or a better understanding of just how much weighing all the options is really necessary. You value your ability to deliberate on issues, and give yourself plenty of time for analysis and reflection, but you make sure you don't waste time when it's not necessary. You see how you can use other head-oriented strengths in combination with your judgment, such as prudence and self-regulation, as well as heart-oriented strengths, such as love and gratitude. You strive toward—although never perfectly achieve—having less personal bias, less stereotyping, and more healthy, logical thinking as you build knowledge and share it with others.

JUDGMENT/CRITICAL THINKING

LOVE OF LEARNING

WHAT　　　WHY　　　HOW

What to Know About Love of Learning

Love of learning means a passion for learning, a desire to learn just for learning's sake. In fact, curiosity and love of learning are among the most closely related strengths in the VIA Classification. They can still be distinguished, though. While curiosity is the motivating force that leads you to seek out new information, love of learning refers to the desire to hold on to and deepen that information. The curious person is motivated by the pursuit of knowledge; the person who loves learning is motivated by the expansion of their fund of knowledge. Where curiosity is often associated with a great deal of energy and a drive to gather information, the lover of learning is often more contemplative.

If you love to learn, then reading one blog post or hearing a two-sentence response to your question is not enough for you. You want to delve into the topic and really learn a new skill or master new material. This might involve reading several books on a topic, taking a formal course, pursuing a new degree or certification, mastering a new trade, or pursuing some topic using a variety of sources. The love of learning can be associated with an enjoyment in going to museums, searching online libraries, reviewing websites rich with information, and watching documentaries and television shows that are educational in nature.

New content and information matter to you. You err in the direction of taking in more information than you can integrate rather than less, not settling for just enough to get by, and aren't satisfied with a shallow understanding of things. You feel genuinely excited about new information. This mastery of new information can result in a variety of positive emotions, including gratitude, joy, pride, hope, and even a sense of peacefulness.

No doubt you are adept at both initiating and directing your learning. In particular, you can direct your learning to help you in your daily life, whether your learning focuses on the nature of relationships, financial matters, or how your community functions. In fact, you are prone to viewing most of your life experiences as learning opportunities; you are enrolled in "the school of life." Problems and setbacks, conversations, social media, and even driving to work are all learning opportunities. When you are learning something new, it is as if a door has opened in front of you, and with it comes a strong desire to keep digging for more information.

WHAT | WHY | HOW

Why Love of Learning Is Valuable

Research findings on the benefits of the strength of love of learning include the following:

- Love of learning leads to the development of a deeper base of knowledge, enhancing competency and efficacy.
- Those high in love of learning tend to do well in school and read a good deal. They are often quiet or introverted. This is not always the case for those high in curiosity.
- Love of learning supports positive experiences that, in turn, may predispose an individual to psychological and physical well-being.
- Viewing a new setback or challenge as an opportunity for learning and growth leads to greater perseverance.
- Love of learning has been associated with healthy, productive aging.

How to Ignite Your Love of Learning

REFLECTING

Consider these questions as you reflect on your strength of love of learning:

- What areas of learning (factual knowledge, people, skills, philosophy, or spirituality) do you find most interesting? What areas of learning do you find least interesting?
- What is it that you love about learning?
- What ways of learning (e.g., reading, experiential, solitary, social) are most/least engaging for you?

- How does knowledge improve your life?
- How does the breadth and depth of your knowledge affect your relationships, from people recently met to people who are close to you?

Meet Katrina M., 24, an elementary school teacher:

I was a good student. I went to what's rated the best school in Colombia, and they really pushed excellence. Then, my parents changed us to another school and I was in the top of the class. Wherever I have gone, books and learning have remained very important to me. Books never fail. If you don't like a book, you can find another one. They're like pets; they never let you down.

I guess what's unique about me is that when other people stop at one book, I keep going. I get five or ten books on the topic. I learn from the books, I learn from Internet searches, and I learn from talking with others about the topic. I love to build up my understanding of a topic.

It's not only books—I learn as much as I can about whatever my passion is. Now my passion is cooking. I practice cooking every day, I watch eight different cooking shows, and of course, I read cooking books and cooking blogs online.

I used to have a passion for computers. I would go to the computer store just to ask questions. Sometimes I'd get someone who was really into it and would answer all my questions with great detail. Eventually I learned how to build computers myself. It wasn't for the money or anything. I didn't want to sell them; it was just so I could learn about them and understand what was really going on.

My passion for learning has run the gamut of many other topics, such as sailing and flying. I plan to get my license in both. I've lived in three different countries, and as I reflect on why, I think it's because I wanted to learn about other cultures as deeply as I could, especially those that are different from my own.

TAKING ACTION

In relationships

- Within one of your close relationships, explore and develop a new hobby or activity that you can learn more about together (e.g., cooking, collecting something, reading the same book, bird-watching).
- Seek out someone with whom you can have an in-depth conversation on a topic of mutual interest or a topic you are interested in learning more about.

At work

- If you like gathering information, researching topics, and learning new things, you are exercising love of learning. You may also seek out opportunities to learn from your fellow co-workers. Consider what wisdom each co-worker has to offer and explore what you can build from that knowledge.

- During a work break, give yourself 5–10 minutes to learn something new on a specific topic that interests you. Set your timer and search the web on this topic.
- When you deeply investigate and study new topics, you are using your love of learning. When this investigation relates to an aspect of your current work projects, this can be a great asset to the organization. Explore with your supervisor how you might best use your love of learning strength at work—maybe take an online class, participate in a free online course, or attain a new certification.

Within your community

- Visit a building or new business in your community and take the opportunity to learn more about it through as many forms of media as you can (e.g., video, reading, website).
- Consider a community topic that is important to you. Spend time learning all you can about the topic, issue, phenomenon, or situation. Then think about how you can use that knowledge to contribute to the community.

Turned inward

- Learn more about yourself, about who you are. Explore the many kinds of strengths you have, where each strength comes from (family background, other relationships, personal experiences, etc.), and the many ways you have used them in your past.

FINDING BALANCE

Underuse of love of learning

Love of learning can sometimes be segmented: maybe you display a significant love of learning for sports and cooking, but zero love of learning for painting and computers. The latter may come across as an underuse of love of learning, especially if the subject matter is important for your job or other parts of your life. In some instances, your underuse of love of learning may simply be a lack of interest or curiosity for the subject.

Underuse can quickly be noticed in intimate relationships. People often show a strong desire to learn about the other person during the dating and courtship phase, but once they enter the commitment phase, the love for learning plummets. They can slowly begin taking their partner for granted, becoming complacent, assuming they know everything there is to know about their partner. Reinvigorating the love of learning about your relationship partner (or those in other relationships) can be a way of sparking, revitalizing, or deepening the relationship.

We caution against assuming that people who didn't obtain a college degree are low in the love of learning strength. In reality, they may not have had the opportunity or resources to pursue it. Many people without degrees continue to read nonfiction and pursue other means of learning for their entire lives. Look at behavior rather than outcomes when reflecting on the love of learning.

Overuse of love of learning

When your love of learning runs rampant, you can come across to people as a know-it-all. There is no topic about which you have

LOVE OF LEARNING

nothing to say, and usually you have so much to say it's as if you're giving a short (or long) speech. The tendency to share information when the people around you have other goals (solving a problem, or even just engaging in casual conversation) can be annoying to others. To be fair, you are enthusiastic about knowledge, about your learning, and perhaps you just want others to benefit from it, but in some situations it will appear to be showing off. When the sharing of knowledge becomes "too much" for the situation, where others begin to have a negative impression of you, that's where it can be labeled as overuse (for that situation). For the recipients, it may be overwhelming and information overload or they may perceive you to be monopolizing the conversation. In these situations, you might not be aware that so much sharing is overkill. Unfortunately, if that becomes a pattern, it is possible that people may avoid interacting with you or try to keep the conversation to a minimum.

Erik K., 43, is a lawyer who shares this about his overuse of love of learning:

> *My sister said I was a pain in the ass to her because I always wanted to tell her the things I was reading. I loved sharing various obscure facts that no one else knew. If she asked me to tell her something, I would give her a book and say, "Read it, read it." She was always very smart, but she was feeling I was always holding how smart I was over her head. I loved sharing my learning with others as well. It was as if I was looking to hear "wow, that's interesting" every time I spoke. I have really had to work hard to avoid acting superior to others because of all the things I knew.*

I also think my biggest weakness is moving certain things into action. I'm really good at figuring out concepts and finding the information I need. The shower is where I have my brainstorm moments, then I will do the research, but oftentimes the ideas stop there. Probably because so many things interest me that I don't want to be focused on one thing, so I don't see things through. I have learned I need to enact other strengths to bring my new projects to the finish line. This takes effort and planning on my part, or setting up a good collaboration with others.

Optimal use of love of learning:
The golden mean

LOVE OF LEARNING

Love of learning motto:

"I am motivated to acquire new levels of knowledge, or deepen my existing knowledge or skills in a significant way."

Imagine this:

You look to every situation as a potential source of learning. When you're alone you learn, when you're with others you learn, when you're stressed you learn, and when you are in the midst of a great time you also learn. You don't get locked into turning everything into learning, though.

You enjoy fun times, you bring kindness and social intelligence to bear when you're with others, and you use zest and perseverance on projects. When you are up against time constraints that might impact your learning pursuits, you use prudence to review how your choices reflect your priorities, and you consider whether love of learning fits in as a central priority for that situation.

You pause to check in with how others are receiving the information you give them and occasionally ask them questions to let them share what they know, such as, "What do you think about that?" You practice observing others while you're sharing your knowledge in order to gauge whether they are engaged or disengaged, open or closed, and truly interested or not. You check in with trusted others to see if you are coming across as superior or balanced.

PERSPECTIVE

| WHAT | WHY | HOW |

What to Know About Perspective

Perspective means the ability to see the bigger picture in life. Perspective is about being able to see the forest as well as the trees, to avoid getting wrapped up in the small details when there are bigger issues to consider. While listening to others, perspective helps you to simultaneously think about life lessons, proper conduct, and what's best for the situation being discussed. This ability to look at systems as a whole, or to think in big terms, helps you to offer good advice.

Even if you haven't faced a particular situation a person is going through and telling you about, you are able to ask the right questions at the right time and apply general life principles to help them. Thus, other people quickly come to you for advice to gain insight and ideas. Those who have perspective tend to possess strong self-knowledge and understand their own limitations.

When you are at your best with perspective, you are quickly able to get to the heart of problems, account for the bigger picture, and offer advice and support for others that is both practical and meaningful.

Perspective and judgment can complement each other. Where judgment is about making sure you have the details that can lead to a good decision, perspective has to do with thinking about the problem in bigger terms. Judgment tends to be a micro strength (focusing on details), whereas perspective veers toward the macro (focusing on the big picture).

WHAT	WHY	HOW

Why Perspective Is Valuable

Research findings on the benefits of the strength of perspective include the following:

- The ability to think in terms of big issues such as death and one's role in the world is more robustly linked to the well-being of older people than are conditions such as physical health, socioeconomic status, financial situation, and physical and social environments.
- Individuals with perspective are valued by others seeking counsel since those individuals help them see the big picture and alternative points of view.
- Perspective plays an important role in applying strengths according to the "golden mean"—the right strength, the right amount of strength, and in the right situation.

- Perspective enables people to learn from mistakes and from the strengths of others.
- Perspective enables people to judge both the short- and long-term consequences of actions.
- Perspective helps to buffer against the negative effects of stress and trauma.

How to Ignite Your Perspective

REFLECTING

Consider these questions as you reflect on your strength of perspective:

- When has looking at a problem from another level been most helpful for you personally and for others around you?
- At times when it was difficult to gain perspective, how did you work to see the big picture?
- Standing on the sidelines and observing can provide perspective, but sometimes it feels like missing the action. How do you strike a balance between observing and participating? Holding back perspective and sharing it?
- What are examples of times when your perspective was easiest to share?
- What have been one or two of your missed opportunities in sharing this strength?

PERSPECTIVE

SPOTTING THE STRENGTH

Meet Jaisong Z., a 42-year-old project manager:

When my sister was going through a divorce, I was the one she kept turning to for advice—not just because I'm a lawyer who knows the legal elements but also for advice on life issues. She struggled to move forward in her life. I would remind her to come back to what mattered most—helping her kids get through it all in one piece, keeping up with her job, and even finding time for herself. She would start worrying about who's going to get a piece of furniture or TV, and I would eventually bring her back to those more important things.

I think perspective has also helped me a lot in my work as a lawyer. I try to look at the bigger picture of what my client is going through and get a sense for how that compares with similar situations I've counseled others on. Then, I share with them what I think might be best for them. I always strive to give them good counsel and explain things thoroughly, in a way that relates to their situation.

I've always been a reflective person. It's not that I don't jump in to do things; it's just that I tend to reflect on my past experiences, what I learned from my parents, and what I've read before I try something. This is the foundation of my approach in my personal and work life.

TAKING ACTION

In relationships

- Monitor times in which you offer good advice in one of your close relationships. Consider the positives and negatives of offering your perspective. How might you improve in sharing (or not sharing) perspective in the future with this person?
- Ask someone you are close to how they find your perspective helpful. When is it not helpful?
- Make note of friends who seem to be struggling in some way. Offer them a different perspective on how they're handling that struggle if you think they will be open to it.

At work

- Approach a co-worker whom you know has been having a conflict or difficulty at work. Offer to help them explore a different perspective, give concrete advice, or simply provide a listening ear.
- For a challenging work project, go outside your inner circle in order to gather the perspectives of multiple sources, such as other co-workers, customers, and the broader community.
- Oftentimes the situation calls for you to look to the future, to envision what might be possible. When you step back to consider this "bigger picture," you are using your perspective strength. Use your perspective to consider your organization's mission/vision statement. As you work on projects, collaborate with your team, and do daily work tasks, keep the mission/vision statement in

PERSPECTIVE

mind. Are your work activities matching the goals of the organization? Would there be a better way to pursue those goals?

Within your community

- Take a look at your community as a whole—not just the geographic boundaries but all the businesses, residences, parks, land, water, trees, animals, and people. View yourself as one small part in this system. Notice and name the character strengths of this community as a whole. Is it a kind and fair community? A creatively curious one? A prudent and brave one?

Turned inward

- Imagine having a conversation with a person who has perspective about a personal problem. Imagine the full dialogue in terms of questions you would ask the person, the back-and-forth of the conversation, and the advice and answers they would provide. This helps you to use your perspective strength to help yourself.

FINDING BALANCE

Underuse of perspective

It's easy to lose perspective in a situation—to get lost in the details, overwhelmed by anxiety or stress, or be inattentive to what's really going on around you.

There are virtually unlimited reasons why you might underuse perspective in a situation—you might not want to help the person, you might not feel worthy or qualified, you might be intimidated or lacking in confidence, or you might be feeling too much emotion or stress to think clearly about the situation. For example, in many family relationships, it's common to return to old patterns and old emotions that immediately limit perspective. To offset that tendency, you might prepare yourself ahead of time. Think about the conflicts in your family and about whether there is a better way for you to respond to them when your family gets together.

Overuse of perspective

Some may say that you can't overuse your perspective, but too much of any strength turns into something else. In the case of too much perspective, it is possible to be overbearing. Sometimes people don't want advice or to be reoriented to bigger issues. Someone who has received a speeding ticket may not appreciate your lecture on the important role of the police in a lawful society. It can come across as you being a know-it-all, trying too hard, wanting to share so much wisdom and knowledge that it falls on deaf ears, or worse, becoming annoying and upsetting to others. For some people who overplay this strength, it appears as if they are trying to become someone they are not—trying to be the wise sage, the inspirational psychologist, or the motivational speaker. Social intelligence can be used to read the feelings and reactions of others to whom you are giving advice, while judgment/critical thinking can help ground you with details and rationality in the given situation.

Some people who try to see the larger picture can also seem too divorced from the world. It may be hard for them to connect with the nitty-gritty details of figuring out a specific problem.

PERSPECTIVE

Other people may turn to the person with perspective when they need help with big issues, such as what to do with their life or whether they're on the right course; they may find the person with too much perspective is the worst source of advice when they are facing concrete problems.

Judy H., 64, a retired professor of counseling, speaks to her overuse of perspective:

I've always been fascinated by philosophy and theology. It took me years to realize that I laid it on too thick with other people. I belonged to a book club for many years. We would all be discussing something important and everyone was contributing to the issue, and then I would just take things in a whole different direction. Everyone would be talking about the conflict between these two characters, and I'd think of something that some wise sage like Lao Tzu or Gandhi said about conflict, and I'd derail the discussion; people wouldn't know how to respond. Someone in the group finally confronted me about it, and I started to realize I did the same thing with the patients I saw in counseling. They were interested in figuring out what to do with their spouse, and I was off trying to teach them about the nature of relationships. Sometimes I think it was really helpful, but at other times I think I was more interested in what interested me than in what would help them. Over time, I've used more empathy for others' feelings and where they are coming from.

Optimal use of perspective:
The golden mean

Perspective motto:

"I give advice to others by considering different (and relevant) perspectives and using my own experiences and knowledge to clarify the big picture."

Imagine this:

Imagine a struggling friend who comes to you. Maybe they've lost their job, they're fighting with their spouse, or struggling with financial problems. You can feel their pain, but you also immediately see the wider perspective that life isn't over, that as bad as things can get, there will be the potential for rebuilding on the horizon. You realize this but know they're not ready for it. You sit with them and listen—listening more than talking. You bravely offer questions that are challenging enough to bring insight but not overwhelm them. You find a way to bring in hope that is not overstated or dismissive of their current suffering. You repeatedly validate and reflect their feelings using your social intelligence and kindness. You check on their resources in the immediate future and offer them ongoing support and counsel.

PERSPECTIVE

VIRTUE OF COURAGE

BRAVERY

PERSEVERANCE

HONESTY

ZEST

Strengths That Help You Exercise Your Will and Face Adversity

The virtue of courage refers to your will—your digging deep to find motivation to accomplish your goals despite challenges arising within you (negative thoughts) and around you (a person who disagrees with you). There is some complexity in attempting to understand the virtue of courage. Courage and bravery are often used to mean very similar things, so you may wonder why courage is considered a virtue but bravery is a character strength. As we describe bravery below, bravery has to do with specific types of actions. You demonstrate bravery every time you do something despite there being risks or your having fears, but you do it anyway because you know it is the right thing to do. The common thread in the three types of bravery we describe—physical, psychological, and moral—is the decision to act for good in the face of risk or uncertainty.

How is this different from courage? In the VIA Classification, *bravery* is about brave acts. Courage is about something broader, an attitude or approach to life that makes a person capable of bravery when it is necessary. The strengths that contribute to this approach also include *perseverance,* because brave action often requires a willingness to stick to a goal no matter what obstacles you face. It includes *honesty,* because a commitment to the truth is essential to being able to engage in good and brave acts. Finally, it includes *zest,* because bravery often emerges out of enthusiasm for life, optimism, and energy. The courageous person in the VIA Classification comes across as forthright and trustworthy even when bravery is not called for.

One final note about courage: fear and anxiety are very important to identifying a person as courageous. Some people experience little anxiety. These people tend to take risks because there is no internal voice telling them not to. It's not unusual for this sort of person to be seen as reckless, impulsive, or even foolish. The courageous person accurately gauges the risks and is appropriately afraid of negative outcomes. They do not act with courage lightly. Their courage comes from a deep will to act that is greater than their fear; in other words, their recognition that the good that may come from their actions outweighs their personal reservations.

BRAVERY

WHAT   WHY   HOW

What to Know About Bravery

To be brave is to face your challenges, threats, or difficulties. It involves valuing a goal or conviction and acting upon it, whether popular or not. A central element involves facing—rather than avoiding—fears. Bravery comes in at least three forms. There's the *physical* form, when you take risks with your body, which is demonstrated by soldiers and firefighters. There's the *psychological* form, which occurs when you face your own mental, emotional, and other personal problems directly. This one often means bravely admitting to and even sharing your vulnerabilities and struggles with others, and, when necessary, asking for help. A third form of bravery is *moral*, to speak up for what is right even if there is opposition. This occurs when you stand up for those who are less fortunate or can't defend themselves, or when you speak up in a group advocating for the rights of the group. It's not unusual for people to demonstrate one form of bravery but not others: the war hero who is afraid to take risks in his or her personal life, or someone who fights for social justice but doesn't confront his or her own anxieties in a relationship.

To be brave does not mean the absence of fear; it means a willingness to act in spite of fear, risk, and uncertainty. Your willingness to act rises above the fear. If the feared situations you face would be regarded as threatening or fearful for others, such as going into a burning building to help someone, this is known as *general bravery*, while if you face situations that are fearful only to you and typically not to others, such as a fear of enclosed spaces, then this is *personal bravery*. Examples of bravery include resisting peer pressure to drink or take drugs, standing up against a bully who's picking on someone younger, facing a serious illness with grace, speaking up for a worthy social cause, or reporting an unethical action at work that might cost you a promotion.

In many instances, the person who acts bravely is unaware they are being brave. It is only after someone points out the bravery with a clear explanation that the person understands and makes the connection between their action and bravery. This demonstrates the importance of strengths-spotting discussed earlier.

With your bravery, you are probably accustomed to heading into the unknown, dealing with ambiguity, and at times confronting risks. Oftentimes, this is part of the terrain of bravery. When you are at your best with bravery, you take action based on your convictions of what is right, and you face fears and opposition that arise along the way.

Why Bravery Is Valuable

Research findings on the benefits of the strength of bravery include the following:

- Bravery helps people tolerate the vulnerability that is part of growing close to others, thereby helping in the formation and maintenance of close relationships.
- Bravery helps to break a prevailing cycle of abuse or injustice.
- Bravery builds resilience as challenges are overcome and active coping skills are built.
- Bravery involves taking both action and risks, two critical ingredients for personal growth and achievement.
- Bravery is speaking up when things are wrong or unfair. Ultimately, such actions can lead to significant long-term benefits, often for the greater good of others. These actions also engender trust.

How to Ignite Your Bravery

REFLECTING

Consider these questions as you reflect on your strength of bravery:

- How is your bravery expressed; for example, by taking physical risks, supporting unpopular positions, being emotionally vulnerable, thinking unconventionally?
- How does bravery lead you in directions that have a positive impact on your life? Negative impact?
- How does bravery cause people to admire you?
- How does bravery cause people to worry about you?
- How does bravery exclude you from certain experiences or opportunities?
- How do you temper your bravery so it does not put you at undue risk?
- How important is bravery to your self-image?
- What motivates you to act bravely?

SPOTTING THE STRENGTH

Meet Reeta B., 28, nurse:

Courage has always been a part of me. It drove me nuts when I saw people in school being picked on or taken advantage of. I couldn't help myself. I would jump into the middle and let the bully know what I thought. I was pretty tough. I was into sports, and no one would mess with me. If I had been petite, I would probably have gotten myself into some pretty bad messes along the way.

This standing up for what I think is right has become a big part of how I operate in the hospital. Sometimes the doctors or other nurses just give bad advice. They don't know all the information, they're rushing around, and they say things that, because I've worked more closely with that patient, I know is a bad idea. I don't just jump in and say, "Hey, you're wrong," but I'll take them aside and ask them to reconsider. Sometimes the person doesn't take it well, but if you put it in the right terms, most people will realize their mistake and we can fix the problem. I think it's an important service I give to my patients.

TAKING ACTION

In relationships

- Consider a close relationship (or a relationship you would like to become close). Use your bravery to express a compliment (something that might generate a positive emotion) for the other person. Focus on the experience for them and not on your nervousness.
- Consider discussing one of your relationship fears (fear of intimacy, fear of your partner leaving you) with your partner. If it seems to be too much to talk with your partner about this, use your bravery to explore the fear in a journal.
- Take note of something you are concerned about with one of your friends, something that is affecting their well-being. Use your bravery to share it with them or to reflect on how you would share it. If you do, be sure to exert other strengths, such as social intelligence, perspective, and kindness that will help you present it well.

At work

- When you are willing to try things that have an uncertain outcome, you are expressing bravery. For example, take on more responsibility with a project, or begin a new project that involves a difficult challenge for you.

- Approach a work task that you have been avoiding or procrastinating on and face the task head-on. Use your bravery to go right toward the challenge.
- Report an injustice, blatant unethical practice, or abuse of power or resources through the appropriate channels.

Within your community

- Focus on the outcome of a brave act you could commit. For example, think of the person you could benefit by helping or remind yourself of the goodness of the action you could take.
- Think of brave role models in your community in order to be inspired and champion noble values and meaningful causes (write, speak out, participate in a protest, join an activist organization).
- Speak up at a community meeting or write about an unpopular idea for a public outlet.

Turned inward

- Tap into your personal bravery by attending to something you are afraid of that most people are not. Use your bravery and your best coping skills, including your signature strengths, to make some progress in managing or overcoming this personal issue.

FINDING BALANCE

Underuse of bravery

Underuse of bravery often means not standing up for what you believe is right in a particular situation, taking the easy way out, or giving up under pressure. The result is living inauthentically. No one is perfectly authentic, and we are all vulnerable to underusing bravery from time to time. A more extreme version of bravery underuse is cowardice and shrinking from fears. In some cases, people underuse this strength because they are unaware of action that can be taken—they are stuck in autopilot and going through the motions of life—and it never occurs to them to act. Of course, a lack of self-confidence can be a factor here as well.

Being brave in one situation does not mean you will be brave across the board or in very different situations. For example, a police officer may demonstrate incredible bravery on the job, but then resist facing his or her own vulnerabilities or weaknesses.

Overuse of bravery

It's not difficult to spot the Achilles' heel of courageous people—they can quickly cross a fine line and be at risk, in harm's way, or to a lesser degree, may come across as pushy, confrontational, or opinionated. For some people, this is part of the allure and pleasure of bravery. This can also take the form of being an "adrenaline junky," someone who's looking for increased levels of risk in order to experience the rush that comes with those activities. Excessive risk-taking can also reflect overconfidence. It can suggest underuse of judgment, when a risk is evaluated inaccurately. This can certainly affect relationships, when the person's partner is left feeling worried or drawn into situations they would have otherwise avoided.

An important part of bravery is doing what you think is right. Usually, there is a time and a place for bravery. An overuse can sometimes occur when a person is pushing an agenda so far that it causes others to respond negatively, reject the idea, or eventually ignore the person and the issue. Prudence is important in planning how to be brave, and self-regulation can be important to being able to pull back when it's clear you've gone too far. Finally, love and kindness for those who are involved will assist in getting the message heard.

Lacey T., 22, a homemaker, commented on the overuse of her bravery:

When I was a kid, I was bullied a lot, and as I got older, I decided I was going to make sure people didn't take advantage of me or other people. I've really had to learn to control myself. I used to just jump into situations where I thought someone was doing something wrong, or blurt out something that made the person feel defensive. I've had to learn to recognize that sometimes I'm the one who's wrong, and even if I'm right, I should be sensitive to the person I'm confronting. I also have to work with these people, or attend class with them, and they deserve my respect. It's a problem, because sometimes I do just rush in and say, "What you're doing is wrong," but I know I need to be tactful sometimes and not make people feel attacked. My reasons don't always keep pace with my urge to act!

Optimal use of bravery:
The golden mean

Bravery motto:

"I act on my convictions, and I face threats, challenges, difficulties, and pains, despite my doubts and fears."

Imagine this:

Imagine you are in a situation at a town hall meeting where a controversial topic is being discussed. The majority of citizens feel one way about the issue. You, however, have a different opinion but are confident it is the right choice, is morally good, and will benefit most. You feel nervous about raising your hand to speak up. You survey the situation and realize it's the right time during the meeting, so you share. You give your opinion strongly, asserting yourself, and you don't attack or demean the other side. You stick with honest sharing, even though it's challenging to offer the truth so directly in this forum. You use perspective, seeing the bigger picture of the town hall, and that you are one part of the whole. When you become aware of your nervousness, you manage it with mindful breathing and maintaining a sense of hope that you are taking a step toward the greater good.

PERSEVERANCE

WHAT	WHY	HOW

What to Know About Perseverance

Perseverance is sticking with things. It means being hardworking and finishing what is started, despite barriers and obstacles that arise. The pleasure received from completing tasks and projects is very important to those who are high in perseverance. Sometimes he or she must dig deep and muster the will to overcome thoughts of giving up. Perseverance involves organizing oneself to support activities (e.g., scheduling breaks and sticking to them, rewarding oneself in small ways along the way), but when all else fails, this strength helps the person to barrel through until the project is done. This helps build further confidence for future successes and goal accomplishment.

Boredom, frustration, and challenges are foes to perseverance but part of the beauty of this strength is to see these as opportunities to learn and as additional challenges to overcome, or at least to ignore them. Failure is more likely to be viewed as a lack of effort as opposed to bad luck, and the emphasis is placed on the importance of having a strong sense of commitment to meeting personal or professional goals.

Your perseverance has two key parts—substantial effort and sustained effort. You will push hard, but like the Energizer Bunny, you can also keep "going and going." When you are at your best with perseverance, you keep your short-term and long-term goals in mind, overcome internal and external challenges without taking shortcuts, maintain a heathy level of energy and motivation to get things done, and enjoy the whole process.

| WHAT | WHY | HOW |

Why Perseverance Is Valuable

Research findings on the benefits of the strength of perseverance include the following:

- Perseverance helps to improve skills, talents, and resourcefulness as well as build other character strengths.
- Perseverance builds self-confidence, a general belief that things can be accomplished in life and that personal control can be exerted so you can perform effectively.
- Persistent people are often seen as dependable—people who follow through on commitments. This contributes to being a valued team member and builds trust that can be a foundation for good relationships. In fact, trustworthiness is one of the most important dimensions on which other people evaluate us.
- Persistent people learn to focus on task completion, not on perfection, thereby developing flexibility and self-control.

How to Ignite Your Perseverance

PERSEVERANCE

REFLECTING

Consider these questions as you reflect on your strength of perseverance:

- When does persevering in a task feel engrossing to you as opposed to a chore?
- What motivates you to persevere?
- What causes you to stop persevering?
- What role do others play in helping or hindering your perseverance?
- When you succeed in persevering, how does that affect how you approach subsequent challenges?
- What other character strengths support your perseverance on projects?

SPOTTING THE STRENGTH

Meet Casey J., 52, an airline pilot:

Perseverance has pretty much defined my life. When I was young, I was discouraged from racing cars. It was something women just didn't do. So, of course, I insisted on learning to race. I don't do it anymore, but I've set three world records in women's racing in groups. A couple of times I've set the record for the most number of women racing in formation together. There was one year when my sister died and I was overwhelmed with grief, and to deal with it I pursued these world records. No one was going to stop me.

During my entire flying career, almost every certifying flight I took was wildly intense. They would say, "You shouldn't be doing this because you're a woman and you're short." It was like this unending bombardment of harassment. I was the first officer, and went through really hard training; I'm quite capable and smart, but the airline training had me at my limit. I heard there's under a thousand female captains in the world, and I basically made it through using pure perseverance.

I might have been born with this intensity, but at some level I always understood that some people are just going to make it through life on good looks or brilliance, and I always knew I was going to do it by working hard. I was a fifth child, and by the time my parents got to number five they said, "Let her be, she's going to do fine." They did the best they could, but they left me to my own devices of being gritty and pushing forward with everything.

For me, a key part of perseverance involves realizing that when something difficult happens, something painful or something that is perceived as awful, it's not "wrong"; it's just part of the process of getting to what you want.

TAKING ACTION

In relationships

- When you experience a relationship setback and feel the urge to pull back from that person, consider instead how you can use this opportunity to move the relationship forward by addressing it directly.

- Consider something positive you have thought about doing in one of your close relationships that you had been putting off (e.g., calling someone, buying someone a small gift, creating something for someone else). Make an effort to start and complete this project with the intention to bring benefit to the relationship.

At work

- Perseverance can help you stick with a project every step of the way until a goal has been reached, despite challenges that may arise. Practice using your perseverance on projects or challenging tasks by committing to give regular progress updates to your colleagues.
- Emphasize effort over perfection. When you find yourself struggling with a project, bring your attention to doing the best you can—putting forth strong effort—rather than focusing on a perfect final outcome.
- Set a new work goal today. List two potential obstacles that may come up and ways that you will overcome them.

Within your community

- Select a role model in your community who exemplifies perseverance, and determine how to follow in his or her footsteps.
- With a community-oriented project, set small goals weekly. Break them into practical steps, accomplish them on time, and monitor your progress from week to week.

Turned inward

- Name a personal issue you would like to address, maybe a bad habit or vice. Consider how you might step away from that vice or bad habit. In other words, what would it look like to "persevere a little bit more" with that issue?

FINDING BALANCE

Underuse of perseverance

Boredom, laziness, and inertia are signs of perseverance underuse. Feelings of helplessness or lack of control are likely to be present to some degree. Some people are quicker to give up than others. This may be the result of too little confidence, or too little knowledge or skill relating to the topic or project at hand. In addition to feeling helpless, the other "h's" that round out what's sometimes called the depression triad—hopeless and hapless (unlucky)—are also likely to accompany underuse.

Underuse of perseverance can be very domain-specific. For some people it may occur more in the classroom, while for others it's in the workplace or in their intimate relationships. This is often a reflection of how confident or in control you feel in that situation.

Unrealistically high expectations can also result in a failure to persevere, so it's important for you to keep those in check. The failure experiences that result from those expectations can undermine confidence in your ability to persevere in the future. It's important to make sure the task is broken down into manageable pieces so you can have experiences of success along the way.

Overuse of perseverance

When your perseverance is too strong in a particular situation, you may be expressing an unrelenting stubbornness to push forward. This can reflect the unrealistically high expectations mentioned for underuse, but in some cases this can achieve the level of an obsession. The wisdom of letting go when it's clear that the goal can't be obtained will help you fight perseverance overuse. An easily relatable example is the man or woman who "overworks," especially at the expense of family, relationships, and self-care.

Some people use so much perseverance in order to keep a relationship going that they don't realize the relationship is toxic or simply no longer viable. The feedback from trusted others is an important way to build perspective and bravery, as well as honesty with yourself, and avoid perseverance overuse.

Margot T., 36, an investment banker, shared about her perseverance overuse:

My tendency to persevere has been at the root of all my successes, but it has its downside. I often find myself on the achievement treadmill, always after the next goal, and not enjoying what's around me. Now that I have little kids, they've taught me some perspective, and I'm not as driven as I once was. It's not all about that next success anymore. I have to wonder if I was driven in part by my wanting to prove myself somehow, by doing things no one else in my family had ever achieved. I have more balance now, but I have to work at keeping my "old me" in check so I'm not relentlessly pursuing something that is not a good choice.

I've also come to realize now that sometimes giving up is the right thing to do. Before I met my husband, I had a couple of pretty bad relationships. I would say now that they were sometimes emotionally abusive. But I kept telling myself that I could make them work, and I even blamed myself when they weren't working, like if I just tried harder I could make it into something good. I've done that with jobs too, not leaving when it was obvious that it wasn't a good fit.

Optimal use of perseverance:
The golden mean

Perseverance motto:

"I persist toward my goals despite obstacles, discouragements, or disappointments."

Imagine this:

Imagine you have a huge, long-term project you are working on for your family or at work. This important project will not be completed without a good deal of perseverance. You use prudence to break the project into smaller parts, leadership to delegate tasks appropriately, hope to keep the vision of where the project is leading you, bravery to face the difficulties, and zest to attend to your natural energy and excitement for the project. Each strength works in tandem with and is activated by your desire to persevere. You remind yourself that the obstacles that come up are a natural part of the process.

HONESTY

WHAT WHY HOW

What to Know About Honesty

When you are honest, you speak the truth. More broadly, you present yourself in a genuine and sincere way, without pretense, and taking responsibility for your feelings and actions. You are a person of integrity—you are who you say you are—and you act consistently across the domains of your life rather than being one way in the community and a completely different way in your family. As a result, you believe you are being consistently true to yourself.

The complexity of this character strength is often revealed when you consider the multiple roles you play in society (e.g., friend, parent, child, spouse, neighbor, supervisor, subordinate, colleague, volunteer, etc.) and how difficult it can be to consistently stick to your values. But because honesty is a *corrective strength* (it can protect us from errors in judgment), it shows up best in situations where the decision must be made between the easy thing to do and the right thing to do.

Honesty is universally valued, especially in close relationships. It is a pillar of healthy communication and intimacy. Honest people honor their commitments. The central role that honesty plays in establishing strong interpersonal relationships leads the honest person to be viewed as trustworthy and dependable.

Being honest is about being authentic. When you are at your best with honesty, you stick with and express who you are—your core character strengths—rather than playing a role that is inconsistent with your values, or allowing who you are to be suppressed. This leads you to present as genuine, the real you, someone whom others can feel they know.

WHAT   **WHY**   **HOW**

Why Honesty Is Valuable

Research findings on the benefits of the strength of honesty include the following:

- Honest people are typically viewed as trustworthy, which contributes to healthy, positive relationships.
- Honesty is linked with improved accuracy of your goals, reflecting your true values and interests.
- Taking personal responsibility for one's actions can lead to a greater sense of control of your life.
- Honesty allows for more accurate self-assessment of your competencies and motivations—to others and to yourself.

WHAT **WHY** **HOW**

HONESTY

How to Ignite Your Honesty

REFLECTING

Consider these questions as you reflect on your strength of honesty:

- How well do you honor your commitments, agreements, and compromises in your personal and professional relationships?
- When you make a mistake, how easy is it for you to take responsibility for it?
- How often do you neutralize guilt by making excuses, blaming, minimizing, or rationalizing the truth away? Are you aware of these processes when they are happening?
- How do you give feedback to others? Is it constructive, direct, or challenging? Do you avoid giving feedback even when people are not treating you as you would like?
- Who is one of your models of honesty? How might you improve on your own modeling of honesty to others?

SPOTTING THE STRENGTH

Meet Camden B., 24, a social worker:

I was surprised at first that honesty came out as my #1 strength, but the more I thought about it, the more it made sense to me. When I was younger, I was never comfortable with the kind of small white lies that people often told. If someone asked me to do something and I didn't want to do it, I would say I didn't want to do it. I wasn't willing to say, "Sorry, I'm busy" or "That sounds like a great idea, but I can't right now." I would just say, "Sorry, I'm just not into it" or something like that. When people say something that bothers me, I've always tended to let them know. You could call me a straight shooter.

What's most important is being honest with myself. When people give me negative feedback, there's a tendency to want to fight them about it, and I've been as guilty of that as anyone. But one of the important lessons I've learned is to take in the criticism and find the truth in it. It might be a partial truth, a glimmer of truth, or completely true, but they're sharing their observation, so there's almost always some truth in there. That was really helpful for me in graduate school. I know other students would get really upset when a professor criticized their work, or they'd write it off, but I really tried to take it to heart. It has helped me do better in my career.

TAKING ACTION

In relationships

- Contact a family member or friend whom you have told a "partial" truth and give them the complete details.

- When someone asks for your honest opinion, give it to them (with a dose of kindness too).
- Write a letter to someone telling them feelings you have for them that you have not expressed before. Share it with that person if you feel brave enough to do so and if your social intelligence tells you they'll likely find it a beneficial experience.

At work

- Provide honest feedback to team members on a project, and be sure to provide critical input when asked.
- When you are speaking with your co-workers, examine your speech for anything less than direct, clear, specific communication. Watch for tangents, disclaimers, exaggerations, avoidance, and minimizations that begin to pull you from a purely honest expression.
- Present yourself and information truthfully. Abide by the expression "say what you mean and mean what you say."

Within your community

- Write about a community issue that you believe has not been dealt with directly and honestly. Consider sharing your writing with others.

Turned inward

- Be honest with yourself. Name a struggle, bad habit, or vice you have avoided facing or talking about. Begin to face this vulnerability with greater honesty.

HONESTY

FINDING BALANCE

Underuse of honesty

It is unlikely that you are completely honest every time it would be the best choice—to others or to yourself. Our minds are quick to deflect blame, protect us from painful feelings, minimize embarrassing truths, and offer clever ways to evade the full truth. We use disclaimers, exaggerations, and rationalization to protect our self-image. In intimate relationships, transparency is the best approach, but in some relationships this may be discouraged, ridiculed, or simply not part of the family or work culture. There is sometimes an unwritten agreement among people to be secretive and withholding in their communications.

There are many social situations in which it's far easier to underuse honesty—to help the situation move forward or to protect the other person's feelings. You need to deploy your social intelligence to determine whether underuse is appropriate in the situation or not and how a balanced expression may best fit. This won't always be clear, but the benefit of considering being more honest is that it will help you think more clearly about when you're holding back to protect someone's feelings or holding back because it seems easier. White lies are very different from habitual lying, telling half-truths, or simply ignoring the subtle denials the mind is capable of creating.

For many people, it is difficult to be direct and very honest. They feel it makes them too vulnerable, and they worry that others will take advantage of them. Sometimes a maladaptive coping strategy develops. For example, for many people with addictions, their motto for operating in life is: "Don't feel. Don't reveal. Don't trust." This form of honesty underuse probably protected them or served them in the past, but it puts limitations on relationships in adulthood and it's important to address it.

In addition, you may make assumptions about another person, as when Jack Nicholson said in the movie *A Few Good Men*, "You can't handle the truth!" However, oftentimes that assumption is an excuse, because in reality we don't feel comfortable telling the truth. When this thought crosses your mind, consider whether you are protecting that other person or protecting yourself.

Overuse of honesty

Modern research has clearly shown that there can be too much of a good thing. Too much honesty and truth-telling can be hurtful and damaging to others. Many times, others are not psychologically ready for the truth. That said, consider whether they may be ready to hear part of a truth or a milder version of it. Too much honesty can make a problem seem bigger than it is or even worsen a problem. The way in which feedback is provided is also an important issue to consider. If it's shared in a way that is too blunt or hurtful for the listener, that can just make matters worse. In other situations, sharing might be a violation of something shared in confidence or the violation of a personal trust.

Javier H., 58, a consultant and public speaker, has this to say about honesty overuse:

> *I really value being honest with others, but I had to learn how to keep from going too far. I know when I was younger I hurt some people's feelings. I was more concerned about letting*

people know how I felt or what I thought than thinking about how they would react. But as I got more mature, I realized that wasn't always necessary. So instead of saying things like "I didn't like that you did that," I'd say, "You know, that hurt my feelings" or try to take responsibility that it was my perception of things. It was a hard lesson to learn, but it has been an important one. I think I'm still as honest as I've ever been, but I've learned that I always have to think about how the person is going to hear it.

Optimal use of honesty:
The golden mean

Honesty motto:

"I am honest to myself and to others, I try to present myself and my reactions accurately to each person, and I take responsibility for my actions."

Imagine this:

Imagine you are striving to be a person of integrity and authenticity. See yourself acting consistently in your relationships, at work, and in your community whenever you can. You tell the truth, you consider others' feelings when you are sharing difficult news, and you are direct and clear in your communications. People trust your word. When you are behind closed doors, you prioritize the same level of honesty and integrity. In your business relationships and in your social relationships, you allow your highest character strengths to be present and to drive your interactions. At times, raw honesty is difficult but necessary. You rise to the occasion, exhibiting bravery and perseverance with your honesty, but also exhibiting kindness and social intelligence in how you express yourself to others. Being honest about your own weaknesses or failings means you take your licks when they're appropriate, and you use perspective to accept that doing so is the right thing to do. Each step of the way on your honesty journey, you have a companion strength in the passenger seat. That strength is kindness.

HONESTY

ZEST

WHAT WHY HOW

What to Know About Zest

Zest means approaching a situation, or life in general, with excitement and energy, not approaching tasks or activities halfway or halfheartedly. People who are high in zest are excited to get up in the morning, and they live their lives like an adventure.

Zest refers to feeling a sense of aliveness and enthusiasm for different activities. The character strength of zest is related to vitality, which comes from the Latin word *vita*, meaning life. In other words, zest helps you feel alive in both body and mind, and participate as fully as you possibly can in life. In this way, the energy of zest is crucial for building good health and keeping strong habits for physical and mental well-being. You certainly don't view life from the sidelines. Your enthusiasm is contagious, in that people who value zest often want to be around you.

This energy carries into different life domains. Zest is often connected with feeling you have found a "calling" in life, often in your work. Zest not only brings pleasure; it also contributes to a sense of meaning or purpose in your life. When you are at your best with zest, your enthusiasm for living is expressed in a balanced way that creates happiness for yourself and others and builds meaningful relationships.

WHAT	WHY	HOW

Why Zest Is Valuable

Research findings on the benefits of the strength of zest include the following:

- You are likely to view your work as a calling in life, in that the work is deeply fulfilling, meaningful, and purposeful.
- Zest is one of the two strengths most strongly connected with happiness.
- Zest is strongly connected with various elements of happiness, including heightened pleasure, engagement, and meaning.
- Zest draws other people in, providing opportunities for developing fun and meaningful relationships.
- Zest is closely connected with the strength of hope, as both are aligned with higher positivity. Zest is more in the moment, but each has an element of looking to the future.
- Zest allows for a fuller expression of abilities, skills, and talents.
- Zest can activate inspiration, motivating people to take on and complete new projects.

WHAT **WHY** **HOW**

How to Ignite Your Zest

REFLECTING

Consider these questions as you reflect on your strength of zest:

- What conditions (people, places, or activities) bring out your zest?
- What conditions put a damper on your enthusiasm or zest?
- How does zest cause positive things to happen in your life?
- How does zest lead you, if at all, in directions that you later regret?
- How do good health habits (e.g., healthy nutrition, exercise, and sleep) set the stage for your zest?
- How does the energy level of others influence the expression of your enthusiasm or zest? How does your energy level impact others?
- Zest is well described as a *value-added strength*, meaning that its moral nature is best revealed when it is combined with other character strengths. Which of your character strengths might combine best with zest?

SPOTTING THE STRENGTH

Meet Pierre M., 42, an occupational therapist:

I've always been excited by every day. I sleep well and wake up in the morning thinking about what the day will bring me. I've always been this way. I was a good kid, very popular, I think because kids always considered me enthusiastic and happy. Some kids made fun of me because of it, but it never bothered me. In fact, I think it has been a real asset for me. I've always been popular in jobs that involved interacting with people. I used to work in an electronics store doing sales, and I think people found my excitement about what I was selling infectious, and they would get excited. I sold well. I would tell people if I didn't think the gadget they were looking at was good, and when I did think it was right for them, they tended to pick up on my enthusiasm about it.

Occupational therapy has been a good career choice for me. I often work with people who are in bad situations. They're sad, they're trying to recover from some physical problem. I think my energy helps lift their spirits sometimes. I try to get them excited about what it will be like to go home again, be more empowered, and be on their own.

TAKING ACTION

In relationships

- Ask your relationship partner about their day. When they share a positive story or success they had, give them an enthusiastic response and express positivity about their sharing more with you.
- In one of your close relationships, spot a character strength in action and express enthusiasm and appreciation for that person's strength.

At work

- It's often the case at work that we are completely focused on getting work done, and not approaching it with enthusiasm. Do something that you already do at work, but with a bit more energy and vigor. Engage your zest for the task by thinking of the positive aspects of the activity.

- Because zest is affected by exercise, go for periodic walks while you are at work, in between tasks. Wear a pedometer to keep you motivated and walking regularly. Less than 5,000 steps per day is considered a sedentary lifestyle, while more than 10,000 steps per day is considered an active lifestyle. Gently increase your steps (and zest) by setting reasonable goals with your step-count.

- Think of ways to make an assignment or task exciting and engaging *before* you undertake it.

- If you find your energy running out, take a break. Engage in a self-care activity, something you enjoy doing. Commit yourself to returning to the task with a brighter outlook.

Within your community

- Approach a task in your community with enthusiasm and energy. See if you can inspire the same emotions in others.

- When you go into your community, express your energy through your outward appearance—an outfit, pair of shoes, and/or accessories that are striking and colorful.

Turned inward

- Exert your energy in a unique way—jump on a bed, run in place, practice yoga or body stretching with a partner, or chase around a child or pet.

- Become enthusiastic about one of your personal qualities. Name the positive quality you see in yourself and take a moment to savor it. Allow yourself to feel excited about how important this quality is to you.

FINDING BALANCE

Underuse of zest

An underuse of zest is easy to spot when someone shows a lack of energy at work, little enthusiasm for a new idea, or a general sense of deflation in their body language. This may reflect fatigue, tiredness, sickness, boredom, lack of interest, even depression, or some other physical or psychological factor. The cause could also be social, such as being around negative or critical people or experiencing overwork. When you notice your attention and excitement level wane, it can be important to evaluate what might account for this. The management of zest underuse involves figuring out the cause. You may be able to correct a lack of zest by boosting your use of your signature strengths (which are generally the highest energy source for you), becoming more physically active (e.g., taking a walk, exercising), being around an upbeat and positive person, or engaging in more self-care.

Overuse of zest

While zestful people can be infectious to be around, the energy can become overbearing in some situations, especially when the zest is particularly strong and constant. Zest overuse can involve poor timing (e.g., it's too early in the morning) or context (e.g., at a funeral home).

Other people can become skeptical of a very zesty person, suspecting their zest is fake or unrealistic, or thinking they are too energetic or enthusiastic. In worst-case scenarios, people want to avoid the person behaving with a good deal of zest. The use of self-regulation, humility, or prudence can bring balance to zest overuse. In addition, when high zest is too much for a particular situation, this energy can be channeled into other areas of interest or brought to other character strengths (rather than simply squashing the zest).

Kerry G., 22, a musician, offered some thoughts on his zest overuse:

ZEST

I've always been a hyper person. People will call me that, and it's true, but it's because my mind goes a mile a minute wondering about things, trying to figure things out. What I wish is that my mind would give me a break sometime. Somewhere along the way I lost the "off" switch.

My girlfriend has brought up the idea that my energy level is sometimes beyond what most people enjoy, and that's gotten me into trouble. Sometimes, it helps me connect with people, but other times I know it's overkill. When I get into these situations, I tend to talk fast, and it can seem almost manic, but I'm able to slow it down. I'm not out of control. I can still relax. I definitely do stand out, though. Sometimes I think people are saying, "What's with Kerry? Why is he always so positive?" But my girlfriend says it's not as bad as I think. And there are some situations when I have tried stupid things—experimenting, you know? I could have been seriously screwed up from some of the things I tried, but I've been lucky. That said, I experience so much joy in my life, and in my music, that I wouldn't want to change it.

Optimal use of zest:
The golden mean

Zest motto:

"I feel vital and full of energy, I approach life feeling activated and enthusiastic."

Imagine this:

Regardless of your current health, imagine you are experiencing a good deal of zest in all aspects of your life. You are happy to be alive. You are grateful for the good that exists in your relationships, health, and all that is around you. You can see the good and positive elements of your health in your body and in your mind. You are able to be active, and this gives you even more energy.

When you encounter difficulties with your health or vitality, you use bravery to face the challenges and perseverance to keep going. You continue to return to pathways that energize you and uplift you each day, even in small daily activities. You find micro-moments of joy and aliveness in your habits, in nature, and in your interactions with others. You minimize your exposure to that which drains your energy, whether that's because of certain foods or drinks, draining relationships, or unnecessary routines. You are tolerant and accepting of those who display less enthusiasm. You maintain a solid level of humor in the moment, and hope and curiosity about your future.

VIRTUE OF HUMANITY

LOVE   KINDNESS   SOCIAL
                               INTELLIGENCE

Strengths That Help You in
One-On-One Relationships

Humanity is one of two virtues in the VIA Classification that have a lot to do with your approach to other people, the other one being justice. Humanity generally has to do with how you connect with people in one-on-one situations. That said, humanity is not limited to one-on-one situations, but situations with more than one other person often also call for using the justice strengths. Humans are born attracted to other people. People who are particularly humane develop that attraction into the ability to feel other people's pain or know their feelings. They know the right thing to say or to do to help other people feel cared for or loved. They go out of their way to help others. Sometimes humane people go out of their way for others even at substantial cost to themselves, and express generosity just because they feel for another person.

Behavior that seems humane but that is performed primarily or exclusively for personal gain does not mark a person as humane. The person who cares for an elderly relative so he will inherit from that relative is not acting badly, but also is not acting humanely. What matters is how a person behaves in general to others, because it is unlikely a person will generally act humanely without a deep connection to other people. The strengths associated with humanity include *love*, *kindness*, and *social intelligence*.

LOVE

What to Know About Love

After millions of songs and greeting cards, love needs no introduction. That said, we want to be clear about how the term is used in the VIA Classification. Love as a character strength, rather than as an emotion, refers to the degree to which you value close relationships with people, and contribute to that closeness in a warm and genuine way. Where kindness can be a behavioral pattern applied in any relationship, love as a character strength really refers to the way you approach your closest and warmest relationships. *Love is reciprocal*, referring to both loving others and the willingness to accept love from others.

Love involves strong positive feelings, commitment, and often, sacrifices. You can experience different types of love: attachment love that parents and children have for one another, companion love or friendship, love for family, and romantic love. Other kinds of love include the love for pets/animals and agape love, also known as spiritual love. The capacity to experience all of these types of love, scientists believe, is rooted in early attachment to other people. Patterns of secure attachment, established in infancy, can show up decades later in adult romantic relationships.

Your love for others is about connection—feeling and offering a positive, warm connection with one or more people. This strength is crucial to developing relationships that nurture and sustain life satisfaction.

When you are at your best in expressing love, there is an easy give and take of positive emotions between you and another, and you feel a bond and closeness in that interaction. Almost everyone experiences and offers love during their lives. In contrast, love as a signature strength means those relationships are at the core of how you see yourself as a person of worth.

WHAT　　WHY　　HOW

Why Love Is Valuable

Research findings on the benefits of the strength of love include the following:

- Love tends to facilitate tolerance, empathy, and forgiveness in relationships, which contribute to the health and longevity of those relationships.
- Loving and secure relationships are strongly linked with longer life and good health.
- It is one of five strengths most associated with enhanced life satisfaction.
- Loving and secure relationships can provide a sense of meaning and purpose in life.

- Love is associated with healthy patterns of communication, such as compromise, and the ability to engage effectively in conflict with others.
- The practice of loving-kindness meditation, in which you cultivate feelings of warmth for yourself and for others, has been shown to boost this strength in addition to a wealth of positive outcomes for the body and mind.

WHAT　　　**WHY**　　　**HOW**

How to Ignite Your Love

REFLECTING

Consider these questions as you reflect on your strength of love:

- Who are the people who matter most to you across each of the domains of your life (friends, family, partners, co-workers)? How do you express love in a healthy way with each group? How does your love express itself differently?
- What are the ways in which you express love to others, and how is it received?
- How well do you receive love? It is often easier to give than to receive, but good relationships are a two-way street. Do signs of love make you uncomfortable or afraid of what others may expect from you?
- Love is often reflected in how we communicate with others, how we express our wants and needs, and how we establish give-

and-take in relationships. It is also reflected in how we listen to and respond to good as well as bad news. Do you celebrate with others in a genuine way when good news is expressed? Do you respond with heartfelt compassion when bad news is shared?

SPOTTING THE STRENGTH

Meet Marcus Y., 27, a graduate student:

I come from a very loving family. I was an only child, and my parents made it clear that they were always there for me. They made sacrifices and supported me as I pursued my greatest hobby, baseball.

When I was recruited to play baseball in college, we all celebrated— my dream was coming true. I never could have expected what was coming next. On my very first day of practice, I blew my knee out. Just like that, my season was over and my heart was crushed. My identity up until then was as an athlete, and I never really explored anything else. Baseball had always given my life a meaningful structure, and without it, I was confused and felt very vulnerable. To make matters worse, I was away from my family for the first time. The people I had always leaned on for guidance and comfort were not close. I could have easily spiraled into a very dark place. But I didn't. Thanks to one person.

The teacher who created the sports and wellness program at my college genuinely cared about every athlete. As soon as I got hurt, he was the person who called my parents and took me to the doctor. He made it his purpose to show warmth and care to his students. He was a constant champion for me throughout my entire recovery, and I knew he truly wanted the best for me. When he died during my sophomore year, the first thing I realized was I wanted to be him. I wanted to show the same love and care to other people that he had showed me. Even now, years later, he still has such an influence on me. He cherished his relationships and I, too, recognize that my close relationships are the most important thing in the world to me.

TAKING ACTION

In relationships

- Journal about loving relationships in general, reflecting on what is most valued in a healthy, loving relationship. Put one of your insights into action.
- Consider the degree to which you are currently expressing love in one of your close relationships. Ask them (and give potential examples) when they feel most loved (e.g., through positive words, physical touch, spending time together, caring acts, gift-giving). Follow their suggestion in some way. If it's challenging for you, put forth some effort as a start, or discuss whether other actions could be a good fit for both of you.
- Carve out some time each week to experience uninterrupted quality time in your closest relationship.
- Offer loving, verbal appreciation for one of your close relationships. Be sure to offer a concrete example or two of why you appreciate that person.

At work

- When you are motivated to do your job well out of care for others, and when you are warm and caring with co-workers and customers, you are expressing the strength of love. You express love by showing a genuine interest in the lives (both professionally and personally) of your co-workers. At your next interaction with a co-worker (maybe in a break room, when passing by their desk, or when getting coffee), pause to show them warmth and offer genuine interest in who they are.

- Consider how one specific part of your job is of value for other people. Appreciate this as an expression of your love.
- Create micro-moments of love. For example, when a colleague shares something good that happened to them, respond in a way that is warm and genuine, and encourage them to share more about the topic or event.
- Go out of your way to offer support to co-workers when you see they are stressed or having a bad day. Give them the gift of supportive words and your honest concern.

Within your community

- Reflect on what it might look like to express more love to your community. Perhaps you already feel love for your neighborhood or city, but what might be one step forward to demonstrate that love by putting it into action?

Turned inward

- The practice of loving-kindness meditation is designed to turn the warm energy and care we may easily give to others toward ourselves as well. There are many books, CDs, videos on YouTube, and practitioners that can teach you the practice. Experiment with a version of the practice that allows you to be gentle and caring toward yourself, especially at times when your inner critic might be strongest.

FINDING BALANCE

Underuse of love

You may find it hard to be warm with others. Often, it's because you've been hurt before, and you're afraid to take that risk. You may also recognize that you're not sure how to express warmth and caring to others. Given how much love can contribute to your sense of security and well-being, you may want to take steps to take that risk. You might want to ask others for whom you have feelings of love how you can make your feelings clearer to them.

You might notice that there are relationships and situations in which you underplay your expression of love or you allow the emotional expression of love to wane, especially as the relationship extends over years or decades. There are probably few relationships in the world that could not benefit from more love expressed through words, actions, or emotions.

You may notice you find it easier to express love with family members, a relationship partner, and friends, but its expression in work and community may be less obvious. It can then be easy to perceive underuse. However, love can be used strongly in these other settings through the expression of warmth, care, good listening, genuineness, and positive interpersonal skills.

The underuse of love also manifests as an imbalance in giving love to others strongly but struggling to receive love as well; in other words, not allowing others to give love in return. Some caregivers tend to wear this as a kind of badge of honor that they are only givers, but fail to recognize this underuse and the negative impact it has on relationships. Love can be viewed as a two-way street in which both the giving and the receiving are of equal value.

Another common phenomenon of love underuse is not turning love inward—toward yourself. This can be reflected in poor self-care or self-management skills, or in being harsh and judgmental toward yourself, especially when mistakes are made.

Overuse of love

An overuse of love means to exert love too intensely for a particular person, maybe because that person doesn't think he or she knows you very well. This kind of overuse can inhibit relationship building. We are not referring to unrequited love, a crush, hero worship, or being a fan in love; these are not true expressions of love since the feelings are in only one direction. What we mean here is an attempt to establish intimacy with someone before they're ready to return that intimacy. In particular, that person may be someone who underuses love, or perhaps they're struggling with your indications of love even though you see your expressions as pretty typical and straightforward. If you truly love the person, though, you'll be sensitive to their difficulties with being loved and move forward more slowly. Giving love to another person when they don't reciprocate can also open you to being hurt or used. With love you need to take risks, but you also need to consider keeping your efforts in line with those being made by the other person.

Sophie T., a 28-year-old accountant, commented on her overuse of love:

What's hard with love is you want to be there for people, but you also need to set boundaries in order to take care of yourself. That's something I'm trying to be intentional about doing. I've had a few experiences where I thought people were taking advantage of me. I sometimes think about that book "The Giving Tree," where the tree loves the boy so much that he lets the boy cut it down, and I've sometimes wondered if that's supposed to be a lesson about how great love is or a lesson about how dangerous loving can be. For the most part, though, I've been able to recognize when a person doesn't have the intentions for a beneficial partnership or interaction.

I also recognize that being really loving toward other people can be overbearing at times. I know that can sound weird, but sometimes my partner thinks it's not real, that I can't be that nice all the time.

I'm realizing that to love her, sometimes I have to give her more space, or let something go without discussing every aspect of it.

Optimal use of love:
The golden mean

Love motto:

"I experience close, loving relationships that are character-ized by giving and receiving love, warmth, and caring."

Imagine this:

Imagine you express a good deal of love in your relationships, and this leaves you feeling fulfilled. You have loving thoughts, experience loving emotions, and you share your love through your words and your behavior. You are thoughtful about the people you love. With your relationship partner, you express love in many ways, such as through physical touch, offering acts of service, affirming and appreciative words, and gift-giv-ing. With your friends and family, you express love by spending quality time with them. When you're with your co-workers, you express love through supportive words, active listening, and supportive actions such as acts of kindness. You feel and, when appropriate, express gratitude for the loving relationships in your life. You also exhibit the strength of fairness in that you not only share love but are accepting and appreciative of the love others give you; you welcome it and allow it to fill you.

KINDNESS

WHAT   WHY   HOW

What to Know About Kindness

Simply put, kindness is being nice to others. As you examine kindness further, a number of important dimensions begin to unfold. Kindness is being generous with others, giving your time, money, and talent to support those who are in need. Kindness is being compassionate, which means to really be there for someone, listening intently to their suffering or just sitting with them and silently supporting them. Such compassion involves a deep concern for the welfare of others. Kindness is also being nurturing and caring to others—to enjoy doing favors for them, to take care of them, and to perform good deeds.

Kindness has a powerful effect on others. Research has shown that if you watch someone else act in an altruistic and kind way that you are likely to go out and also be kind and altruistic. Kindness in its purest form occurs when there is true altruism, when you are kind without any hidden agenda or expectation of benefit in return—when you are doing it just to help.

Despite the distinction between them, kindness and love frequently go together, and it's not uncommon for a person high in one to be high in the other. Kindness can be distinguished from love in that the character strength of love has more to do with intimate relationships, whereas kindness is a more general strength, involving reaching out to positively impact people beyond your close circle. Unlike love, the goal of kindness is not necessarily to achieve intimacy and security; it is to make others feel cared for.

If you are high in kindness, it is clear to you that kindness is other-oriented, a strength that aligns with your having a personal ethic of responsibility to care for the welfare of others. You are especially tuned in to the needs of others and are willing to act quickly when someone else's needs become apparent. In many cases, your actions are instinctive and automatic as you put the other person first and figure out a way to lend a helping hand. When you are at your best with kindness, you show a balance of directing kindness toward yourself and toward others.

WHAT   **WHY**   **HOW**

Why Kindness Is Valuable

Research findings on the benefits of the strength of kindness include the following:

- People who give to others, in small and in large ways, tend to be happier as a result.
- People who are consistently kind and giving tend to be healthier and live longer than their less generous counterparts.

- Kind people are often likable to others, which can provide opportunities to develop meaningful relationships and love.
- Kindness directed inward (self-compassion) can contribute to higher self-esteem, less anxiety and depression, and greater life satisfaction.
- Random acts of kindness have been connected with a range of benefits, including greater positive emotions, lower negative emotions, greater well-being, and higher peer acceptance (popularity).

How to Ignite Your Kindness

REFLECTING

Consider these questions as you reflect on your strength of kindness:

- What are some ways you have observed the expression of kindness and compassion by different people in different situations?
- How are your kind acts received by others?
- Do you find that your personal style of expressing kindness focuses on certain aspects of kindness (generosity, emotional caring, niceness, or compassion)?
- In what situations do you find kindness easy to express?
- In what situations do you most struggle to express kindness?
- What character strengths best support your expressions of kindness?

SPOTTING THE STRENGTH

Meet Cheryl T., 48, a business executive:

Kindness is in the fiber of my being, so I don't think about it. It's just my natural response to the world. I felt misunderstood a fair amount by my parents. It was hard to get them to recognize me. So it's always been a big deal for me to recognize people for who they are. I had a neighbor when I was little—I guess I was ten or so—she was a special educator. She sort of took me under her wing, I don't know why. For some reason she saw something in me and took me to work with her. She worked with kids, and it inspired me to volunteer to work in a camp for children with disabilities in high school. I could sit with kids in a lot of pain, and I could break through in a nonverbal way, which is something a lot of the volunteers had a hard time doing.

I try to be kind whenever I can. When something affects you in a positive way, why are you not telling them? I think being kind greases the wheels a little. On a daily basis, I'll tell people they have a great smile, and that changes the tone of an interaction. I'll say that's a really brave thing you did, and I think that that will have a positive impact in the world.

This is revealing about me. My relative had an affair with this woman. This is many years ago; I was twelve or something. He ended up with her, and he was dying and having a horrible, painful death. She stayed with him through it. She was sitting in front of me at the funeral and had been there for him so much. I leaned forward and said, "I can see why he loved you so much." She began to cry. It was a bit risky for me, but I felt it was important to attempt to acknowledge her feelings in the moment.

TAKING ACTION

In relationships

- Consider how you might be generous in one of your relationships. Remember that generosity can involve money but doesn't have to—you can also be generous with your time and with your talents.
- Ask someone you are close to how you can best show kindness to them in a way that they would appreciate.
- Surprise someone you are in a close relationship with by offering a random act of kindness—for example, plan a weekend getaway, cook a dinner, or help them with part of their routine or chores.

At work

- When you show compassion for others by being a good listener, helping others, or simply doing nice things, you are expressing kindness. Express kindness at work by doing something you know will be helpful for a co-worker or client. Go out of your way to make their job a little bit easier.
- While getting a morning cup of coffee at your local coffee shop, purchase a second cup "to go" for one of your co-workers. Alternate the extra cup between your co-workers. If a co-worker has been unkind to you, consider including them in the rotation.

Within your community

- Offer one or more random acts of kindness in your community in an anonymous way, such as paying someone's parking meter or cleaning up an area of a park or around a community pond.

- Offer deliberate kind acts to neighbors in your community, such as helping a neighbor in need with their lawn, with snow on their driveway, with their groceries, or with their pet.

Turned inward

- Practice self-kindness, commonly referred to as self-compassion. You should be thoughtful about your own suffering and manage your self-judgments. You can be honest with yourself while maintaining a kind and understanding approach. This means letting go of perfectionism and giving yourself a break for mistakes that aren't that serious.
- Track your kind acts. Research shows it can be beneficial to count your kind acts each day or each week. This helps to generate awareness of the strength as well as generate new ideas and behaviors.

FINDING BALANCE

Underuse of kindness

The general underuse of kindness is obvious—someone who isn't generous with their resources, someone who is uncaring toward and lacking empathy for someone who is suffering, and someone who is mean-spirited in their interactions. Somewhat less obvious is to imagine yourself lost in your head due to busyness or high stress and completely disregarding the person who is needy, overwhelmed, or crying for help. The enemy of kindness is indifference. However, someone who is not going out of their way to be thoughtful isn't always underusing kindness. No one can always focus on being kind to others—if you did, you might end up feeling quite drained.

Some people are kinder to people they don't know as well, as if they want to make a good impression, than with people they feel most comfortable with, such as a spouse or family member. This paradox is also evident when a child is less kind toward their parents than other people. The reverse can also play out, when people are unkind to strangers, oftentimes those who are different from them in race, religion, country of origin, sexual orientation, education level, and so on.

Everyone is vulnerable to underusing kindness. It's important for every person to identify the settings in which they are particularly kind and those in which a higher dose of kindness would be important.

Overuse of kindness

The most obvious circumstance in which kindness is overused occurs when the person gives so much to others that they have little left for themselves emotionally. The person may end up feeling like a martyr. Undoubtedly, they see themselves as being kind, but this sort of giving until there is little left for themselves often indicates emotional issues that the person will need honesty and perspective to address. For one thing, giving too much away reduces the ability to be kind when it's needed in the future.

A person can also give so much that it appears intrusive. For example, someone you've been giving support for a temporary problem may feel intruded upon if you don't "get the message" when the problem is resolved and they don't need the support anymore. It can be awkward to tell a kind person who is offering to help or be generous with food or money to stop giving.

Some people are particularly good about offering kind acts to people around them, such as small favors, compliments, gifts, and other help, but as with the character strength of love, they find it difficult to receive anything in return. In other situations, the person who offers repeated kindness might expect something small in return, but because the other person doesn't respond with a kindness, the person offering kindness may feel as if they are being taken advantage of or underappreciated.

These examples may lead to another type of kindness overuse that has been called "compassion fatigue." This is particularly common among practitioners in the helping professions such as healthcare. It occurs as a result of giving so much beyond one's limits and resources that the person can feel drained or burned out.

Chloe A., 33, a doctor, had this to say about her overuse of kindness:

My wanting to be kind can mean that I lose myself if I'm not careful. For example, my sister was very strong-willed, and there was a lot of conflict between her and my parents growing up. I felt really bad for them all, but especially for my parents. As a result, I never wanted to be a burden to them. I remember when my father got transferred and we were going to have to move. My sister had a major fit. My dad started crying about it, and I remember saying to him, "I'll be fine." The reality was I had good friends that I was leaving, and I had no idea if I was going to be fine. But I couldn't put more burden on him. I became the supporter for everyone in the family—I did all I could to empathize with them and didn't attend to my own needs. In the end it worked out, and I admitted to my parents years later that I was really sad when we moved. This has been a recurring pattern for me, especially in my intimate relationships.

Sometimes I forget myself in the mix, and I expend myself too much to others, especially in my job, and it ends up not being good for me. I feel out of sorts in those situations. It seems like it's something I'm always going to be vulnerable to.

Optimal use of kindness:
The golden mean

Kindness motto:

"I am helpful and empathic and regularly do nice favors for others without expecting anything in return."

Imagine this:

Imagine you are in a situation with someone who is seriously suffering. The suffering is partly their fault. You know they need your help, and you decide to give them your time. You bring them a home-cooked meal and you eat with them. You sit and listen to them, supporting their feelings, providing a warm and trusting presence. You see their true suffering and validate it. You let them know if you've been in a similar situation and that eventually it became all right. You offer some advice, but most of all you focus on listening and empathizing. They share their appreciation for you, and you acknowledge that gratitude and take it in. You reflect on ways you can offer support in terms of kind acts over the coming week while also considering your family and work obligations as well as your own self-care. You agree to give them more support without overdoing it. Later, you celebrate with them when things get better.

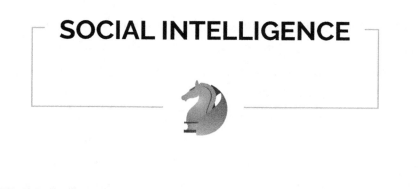

SOCIAL INTELLIGENCE

| **WHAT** | WHY | HOW |

What to Know About Social Intelligence

When a person knows what makes other people tick, he or she is displaying social intelligence. They're aware of the motives and feelings of themselves and others, and how to fit into different social situations. They can feel comfortable and say the right thing whether they're in the boardroom or the janitorial room, in a school setting or at a construction site.

Social intelligence involves not only being aware of feelings, but expressing emotions appropriately (or deliberately not expressing them if that's appropriate). This awareness and social adeptness build relationships with others. Social intelligence helps people "read" others and situations well, and quickly "size up" social nuances and the things that have been left unsaid. Empathy, the capacity to feel another person's feelings, is an important component of good social intelligence.

If you are high in social intelligence, you are accustomed to noticing both the verbal and nonverbal levels of communication by others. You pay attention not only to what is said but how the person said it. Did they have an angry, sad, happy, or fearful expression on their face? Did they look away or make good eye contact? Was their tone of voice forceful and direct, soft and gentle, or shifting around in intensity? You also ask yourself, "What was left unsaid in that conversation? Did the person leave out an important part of their opinion? Did they seem distracted, disinterested, or fully engaged in the conversation?"

When you are at your best with social intelligence, you track your feelings and the feelings in the room and respond appropriately and smoothly in the situation. You are flexible and can shift your responses and style of interacting as needed.

WHAT	WHY	HOW

Why Social Intelligence Is Valuable

Research findings on the benefits of the strength of social intelligence include the following:

- Social and emotional intelligence help in negotiating successful transactions with other people, whether in social or business situations.
- Social intelligence contributes to a high level of comfort across a variety of social situations, opening up opportunities for meeting new people and participating in new experiences.

- The ability to recognize feelings both in yourself and in others has been connected with better mental and physical health, work performance, and social relationships.
- The ability to recognize and respond to differences between others in their moods, temperament, motivations, and intentions contributes to establishing trust and helps in building relationships.

SOCIAL INTELLIGENCE

WHAT	WHY	HOW

How to Ignite Your Social Intelligence

REFLECTING

Consider these questions as you reflect on your strength of social intelligence:

- What are the social situations that have had the most positive outcomes for you, and how did you positively influence the interactions?
- When has it been helpful for you to double-check your "read" on situations? How did you do the double-check?
- In what situations has it been most effective for you to share your emotions directly? In what situations has it been best to hold back your observation of others' emotions?
- What other character strengths help you to be more socially intelligent?
- When has your social intelligence use gotten in your way?

SPOTTING THE STRENGTH

Meet Jennifer B., 43, a practicing psychologist:

I've always been very attuned to people and their needs and feelings. Maybe this comes from my father, because he was a really good "people person." He could strike up a conversation with anyone at any time, and he seemed to always make people feel at ease and normal when he was talking to them.

I'm that way too, although sometimes I gently ask people how they feel. This gets them to open up more. I've gotten a lot of reinforcement over the years that I'm a good listener. Now, I even work to develop it. I look very closely at people's faces and their body language and try to figure out what is going on with them. I'm sort of known in my office for asking people "Are you doing OK?" and many times it turns out there's a problem they're struggling with.

The same thing when I'm in group situations with my friends. I try to figure out how each person is doing. If I think there's someone who's not fully involved or enjoying the experience, I'll go out of my way to reach out to that person and include them. A lot of times at parties I'm in the corner just talking with one person I thought was on the periphery.

TAKING ACTION

In relationships
- When you find yourself in a relational argument you have been in before, attempt to find at least one positive element in the other person's comments and opinions.

- Ask someone close to you what they most appreciate about the way you interact with them. Also ask them what they would most like you to do differently.
- Withhold a powerful and decisive argument that would win a discussion but might hurt someone's feelings.

At work

- Make a point to empathize with one of your co-workers who seems to be upset, stressed, or having difficulty with something in their life. Gently ask some questions, and check in to see whether they are comfortable sharing with you. Be sure to spend more time listening than speaking and, if appropriate, offer emotional support.
- Start a conversation with someone whom you normally would not say much more to than typical pleasantries. This person might be an office clerk, a janitor, the employee in a corner cubicle, or a new employee. Ask about them, what matters to them, or how their day or week is going. Express concern when they seem stressed or celebrate when they share positive emotions or stories.
- Express a feeling of frustration, disappointment, or nervousness in a healthy, direct way that someone at work can understand and grow from.

Within your community

- Attend an uncomfortable community event as an active observer and comment on it to the group without any judgments.
- At a community outing or just walking around a local park, take notice of someone who seems alone, unhappy, excluded, or cast aside. Use your social intelligence to approach them and start a conversation.

Turned inward

- Evaluate one or more of your emotions in a complex situation. Consider the benefits to yourself in sharing those emotions with others.

FINDING BALANCE

Underuse of social intelligence

The underuse of social intelligence might come across as naïveté, as thoughtlessness, or as emotional insensitivity. In some of these cases, the person is innocently unaware of the social complexity around them, or is just inexperienced with interpreting social complexities. In other cases, an individual might be tired, bored, resistant, uninterested, or overly self-involved. Many people struggle with the emotional skills that define this character strength, such as the ability to identify the different ways that sadness, anxiety, anger, or shame manifest, how they're experienced and triggered in the body, how they are expressed in a balanced way, and the thoughts and behaviors that are connected with each feeling.

The range of possible social situations is virtually unlimited, so people will discover they have more comfort and grace in some situations than in others.

Overuse of social intelligence

If your awareness of what motivates others becomes too high, you may find yourself becoming overly cautious or inhibited. You can overanalyze situations, spending too much time thinking about what others in the situation are thinking and feeling, to the point of missing opportunities for yourself. This can be interpreted as being too sensitive or too much in your own head rather than the situation. Another element of this strength's overuse is seen in those who are exquisitely empathic. These individuals become too focused on the pain and suffering of others, which can lead to depression, or feeling overwhelmed or burned out.

Mark W., 22, is an assistant coach in an athletic department who offers some insights into his overuse of social intelligence:

> *Sometimes I become too invested in how everyone else is feeling. I don't have a good time because someone else is having a hard time, and I feel like I have to explore it with them. I used to sometimes push people to share with me, and I've learned that's not a good thing. It's good to be able to figure out what other people are feeling, but there have also been times when I've realized people just want to be left alone with whatever they're struggling with. If I get that feeling, I've had to learn to say, "Listen, just know I'd be happy to talk to you," and move on.*
>
> *Also, I tend to pick up on little comments people say, inflections in their voice tone, or a shrug in their body language. I immediately try to figure out what it meant. Sometimes this is helpful in picking up on someone's feelings, but other times it drives me nuts because I can't figure it out and I waste my time thinking about it.*

Optimal use of social intelligence:
The golden mean

Social intelligence motto:

"I am aware of and understand my feelings and thoughts, as well as the feelings of those around me."

SOCIAL INTELLIGENCE

Imagine this:

Imagine you're invited to a party where you don't know anyone but the host. You tune in to your initial feelings as you walk in the door, ready to be friendly and sociable, ready to attempt to connect with others. You know that your zest and humor will also be important to use in a socially intelligent way. At the moment, though, it's bravery that is most needed. You make eye contact with each person you meet, smile, and nod your head. You ask someone where the host is so you can offer your gratitude.

As you politely grab a drink and a snack, you step back with your perspective to survey the room as a whole. You can tell the mood is casual rather than serious, and more playful than intimate. There is also an air of kindness that is palpable. You feel ready to interact. You make an effort to strike up conversations with three or four different people. Your sharing is a blend of playful humor with professional chatter and interesting life observations. You listen well. After the party, you take notice of the ways in which you "read" the situations and the people, identifying those conversations that seemed to go well and those in which you struggled more, trying to determine why that happened in each interaction.

VIRTUE OF JUSTICE

TEAMWORK   FAIRNESS   LEADERSHIP

Strengths That Help You in Community or Group-Based Situations

J ustice is the second virtue that is specifically about how you interact with other people. Humanity had to do with our personal relationships with others. The strengths associated with humanity tend
to emerge out of our attraction to and feelings for other people. They
are more emotional in their origins, though they often lead to deep
thought about the other person's feelings, needs, and desires.

Interpersonal relationships are not always one-on-one. We also exist
in groups, and so the strengths of justice have to do with how we navigate the competing goals and intentions of people in groups. Where
humanity is about me and you, justice is about me and "you all."

Sometimes, the strengths of humanity and the strengths of justice can be in conflict. We may know, for example, that one member of a group wants a certain reward more than anyone else in the group wants it, but another member deserves it more. We can feel sympathy with the first member, but also recognize that for the other members of the group to feel good about the experience, the reward has to go to the second member. Justice is often a balancing act of many forces, and so is often difficult to achieve. The person who is high in justice can be humane, but also knows that the good of the group must sometimes take precedence over humanity. At the same time, sometimes humanity should take precedence, as long as the group accepts the wisdom of doing so.

The justice strengths are especially important in situations that can create a healthier group or healthier community that you are involved in. The strengths of justice include *teamwork*, *fairness*, and *leadership*.

TEAMWORK

WHAT **WHY** **HOW**

What to Know About Teamwork

Teamwork means that in team situations you are committed to contributing to the team's success. The team could be a work group or a sports team, but it could also refer to your family, marriage, or even a group of friends working on a project together. Teamwork extends to being a good citizen of your community or country, and more broadly to a sense of social responsibility for particular groups of people or even all of humanity. In other words, the person high in teamwork applies a certain way of acting in whatever context they consider themselves committed to the good of the group as a whole. Most commonly, however, this strength refers to your being a dedicated, reliable, and contributing member to your small group or team.

Those high in teamwork have a sense of identification and obligation that stretches beyond them to include family, friends, co-workers, neighbors, etc. An important element of teamwork is working for the good of the group rather than for your own personal gain. You're a trusted member who pulls their own weight, and doing so gives you a strong sense of satisfaction. However, healthy teamwork is not blind obedience to the team; it involves the exercise of informed judgment in the interest of the whole.

When you are at your best with teamwork, you thrive in working in the group (rather than alone) and strive for the betterment of the group or community. You feel connected to others and are confident that the group will be more successful when everyone contributes.

WHAT	WHY	HOW

Why Teamwork Is Valuable

Research findings on the benefits of the strength of teamwork include the following:

- Those high in teamwork elicit and experience a higher level of social trust and have a more positive view of others.
- Teamwork fosters a feeling of connectedness and enhances meaning through shared purpose.
- Teamwork contributes to feeling engaged in work, developing high-quality connections with others, and being creatively involved in the group process.
- Seven team roles that can be identified through our character strength profiles include idea creator, information gatherer, decision-maker, implementer, influencer, relationship manager, and energizer. People vary in terms of which roles align best

with who they are, and greater life satisfaction is associated with the degree to which a person fills the role that is most optimal to them.

- Teamwork is one of the strengths most associated with sustainable behavior, which is defined as behavior that aims to protect the social and physical environment.

WHAT **WHY** **HOW**

How to Ignite Your Teamwork

REFLECTING

Consider these questions as you reflect on your strength of teamwork:

- What is most gratifying to you about being part of a team?
- What is most challenging for you about being part of a team?
- In what circumstances do you prefer to work alone rather than work in a group?
- How do you feel and act when you carry more than your fair share of the weight for a team?
- How are your needs for recognition and appreciation achieved when you are part of a team effort?
- How does teamwork extend into your personal life; for example, parenting, family, partner, friendship?

SPOTTING THE STRENGTH

Meet Angela B., 51, a corporate executive:

> *I work in an environment where teams are regularly organized for specific projects. For any one project, it's possible that most of the people have never met before. We can have different styles of working, and different assumptions about how to best move the project forward. It can be a real challenge, but it's a setting where I really shine. I find the challenge stimulating, and love figuring out how to take a group of people who have never done this before and help them become a team.*
>
> *That means being very supportive and recognizing that some of what happens has to be about building the team and getting to know each other, but also always keeping your eye on the goal. I know it has been a good experience when everyone walks away feeling like they've contributed, they've been valued.*
>
> *My team-building skills are one of the most important things about me as a person, and it's definitely something I know others value it in me, and it's something that's been helpful to me in my career. People who know me are happy when they hear that I'm going to be working with them. I'm not going to be someone who slows things down or stirs up trouble, or tries to grab credit. I'm really interested in everyone in the team succeeding.*

TAKING ACTION

In relationships

- Consider how you and your intimate partner are a "team" who can work together to solve problems. Approach your next challenge with this perspective.

- Examine an event from your past in one of your relationships where you used partnering to the benefit of the relationship. Consider what you can learn from that experience to use in the future.
- The next time someone close to you conveys that they are having a problem, ask them if the two of you can approach the problem together, as a team, and brainstorm, talk it through, and take action in some way together.

At work

- When you enjoy sharing responsibility with others and working with others, you are exercising the strength of teamwork. Express teamwork at your next team meeting or work project by contributing your thoughts and ideas to the group to help with a project or goal. Coax ideas out of others too.
- Examine the tasks facing your team at work. Offer to help with one of the elements of a task that seems to be overlooked or that a colleague is struggling with.
- Validate the successes and acknowledge the character strengths of others on your team; for example, "Jacob, I'm really impressed by how quickly you connected with our new customer. That will really help our company's bottom line. You used good social intelligence to empathize with them and showed you understood their concerns. Then, you showed strong perseverance by sticking with them over the weeks to bring them to sign the contract."
- Savor a positive team interaction from the past by replaying it in your mind. Share it at a team meeting.

Within your community

- Volunteer weekly for a community service project in your town.
- Participate in service learning programs (working with others for social good) that show positive outcomes for the larger community.

Turned inward

- Name a life challenge. Take on a mindset in which you consider yourself your own best partner to face the challenge, come up with new ideas, and activate your strengths. Use journaling to explore this in a conversation with yourself.

FINDING BALANCE

Underuse of teamwork

"Going it alone" with a project is one example of teamwork underuse. Sometimes this occurs because you believe it's easier and more straightforward to do the task or project yourself. The center of the word "collaborate" is "labor," which serves as a reminder that working together does take some effort. A worse case of teamwork underuse occurs when a member sits back and allows other people to do the majority of the work. This choice might be due to laziness, a lack of confidence or skill, or uncertainty about how to deal with more assertive team members. In these cases, the underuse of teamwork can appear to others as selfishness or too much independence, or too much focus on personal goals over communal goals.

Overuse of teamwork

Too much teamwork in a given situation can lead to dependence on others to get things done. This might emerge as a loss of individuality, and team members may not feel comfortable challenging the rest of the group. If you place too much emphasis on teamwork, you might lose sight of the value of your own contributions, and the team can fall prey to groupthink, assuming that certain decisions are the best just because they're the most popular. A good team member should be ready to challenge the group.

Evelyn J., 81, is a retired manager who shares her thoughts on the overuse of teamwork:

> *I have sometimes wondered if I could have been more successful if I had been more self-reliant, if I had exerted a bit more independence. I've seen people succeed who took credit for other people's work or stole other people's ideas, which, in the end, wouldn't have felt as good. But I probably could have done parts of some projects on my own and then shared them with my teams.*
>
> *There were definitely times when I was so reliant on the team in my work, checking in on every little thing I did, that I probably not only annoyed some people but I was ultimately less productive. When I think about it, I was not just annoying, but I felt I could not move forward with my work without the input of others. And sometimes it worked the other way. I felt offended when colleagues moved ahead with their part of a project without consulting me.*

Optimal use of teamwork:
The golden mean

Teamwork motto:
"I am a helpful and contributing group and team member, and feel responsible for helping the team reach its goals."

Imagine this:

Imagine you are participating in a strong, interactive, engaged team. The workload is fairly distributed, the optimism is high, and the team members, including you, want to be around each other, helping each other. What do you notice about the interactions on this team? How are you contributing to it?

Notice the confidence and trust that you have for the other members. Notice the appreciation you have for each person. Be sure to share that appreciation with the other members.

What are the character strengths of the different team members you are observing in yourself and others? How do you see leadership, fairness, honesty, and kindness expressed?

FAIRNESS

What to Know About Fairness

Fairness is treating people justly, not letting your personal feelings bias your decisions about others. You want to give everyone a fair chance, and believe there should be equal opportunity for all, though you also realize that what is fair for one person might not be fair for another. Unfortunately, it is not always easy to judge the fair thing to do, so fairness as a personal strength requires the ability to think clearly about what is morally right and wrong. Fairness encompasses the moral rules that a person uses to decide that something is fair as well as the fairness of their decisions.

Fairness tends to involve two types of reasoning. "Justice reasoning" emphasizes logical analysis of what is objectively right and wrong. "Care reasoning" is more emotional, when a decision about what is fair is based, at least in part, on empathy and understanding the perspective of others.

Fairness also involves the belief that everyone's opinion counts, whether or not they share the same opinion. Compromise, compassion, and a sensitivity to social justice are elements of fairness as it relates to understanding and connecting with others. When you are at your best, you use your fairness to actively work to establish equity and respect for all.

WHAT　　　　**WHY**　　　　HOW

Why Fairness Is Valuable

Research findings on the benefits of the strength of fairness include the following:

- Fair-minded individuals are more likely to engage in positive, prosocial behaviors and less likely to engage in illegal and immoral behavior. They tend to focus on whether their behavior will have a direct negative impact on others.

- Fairness is enhanced by the ability to take on the perspective of others. The ability to deliberate logically over issues of right and wrong is less central but can also be important.

- A sensitivity to issues of morality and justice increases self-reflection and self-knowledge. Having a good moral compass enables you to navigate conflictual situations more effectively.

FAIRNESS

How to Ignite Your Fairness

REFLECTING

Consider these questions as you reflect on your strength of fairness:

- How is your strength of fairness expressed at work, at home, and in the community?
- What are the circumstances in which it is easier or harder for you to compromise to try to achieve a fair outcome for everyone?
- In what situations have you received feedback that you have acted unfairly? How did you handle the situation?
- What emotions do you experience when you perceive an injustice is occurring to others? How does that emotional tendency affect your ability to be fair?
- How do you reconcile your sense of fairness with the reality that "life is not fair"?

SPOTTING THE STRENGTH

Meet Lisa N., 35, an office manager:

> *I never realized how important fairness was to me until the people in my office used the VIA strengths in a team-building exercise. The people I work with had to choose which of the strengths best described*

me, and their number one choice was fairness. I have to say it made me feel proud. I do think it's very important to me that everyone who works under me knows I'm going to treat them equally, and I'm glad they recognized it.

I see a lot of supervisors who take advantage of their workers, or expect more of them than they expect of themselves, or play favorites with some people over others. I just don't think that's right. I really try to make sure everyone who works for me will feel like I'm going to judge them according to their work, and if they don't think I am, then they feel comfortable talking with me about it and I will take in their feedback. That's just the way it should be.

TAKING ACTION

In relationships

- Consider ways to be fairer with friends and family, such as thinking about the amount of quality time you spend with each person and making adjustments accordingly.
- Include someone in a conversation who is typically excluded from groups or is a newcomer.
- Support others in exploring their beliefs and perceptions about people from diverse backgrounds.
- Invite different viewpoints when approaching a problem.

At work

- Take a step to make your workplace more inclusive, encouraging, or supportive of others. Think broadly. You could give more attention to a shy or introverted person, arrange the space to make it more accessible to people with disabilities, or put up signs or posters that emphasize the concept that "every worker matters."

- Involve others in decisions that affect them and allow them to disagree with your ideas and assumptions. Invite their ideas for other ways to approach the decision.

Within your community

- Serve on or consult to the board of an organization that offers underprivileged people a level playing field.
- Write a letter to an editor or speak up on an important issue concerning social justice.
- Work to ensure that policies and procedures for handling complaints and problems in your community are fair for all.

Turned inward

- Be fair to yourself by examining the amount of time you spend focused on your own health and self-care versus time spent focused on helping others. Take action based on what is fair for both you and others.

FINDING BALANCE

Underuse of fairness

Too little fairness in a particular situation can lead to your playing favorites for certain people when you are making decisions. While some detachment can be helpful in striving to be fair, such as a mild emotional detachment to ensure you are not favoring your own children over others' children, moderate or severe detachment can be viewed as callous toward the needs of others. In some cases, the underuse of fairness can merely be an oversight, or a tendency to express it strongly in one setting (e.g., with your family) but underplay it in another (e.g., at work). In the workplace and other settings, workers can become complacent about unfair policies or procedures and come to accept "that's just the way it is here." In families, the perception of unfairness can be especially troubling. Children (as kids or adults) will experience times that they felt their parents favored one sibling over another or they were unfairly treated. Similar patterns play out among employees and students in terms of how they view their supervisor or their teacher is treating them versus others.

In some cases, fairness might be withheld for revenge, when you treat someone unfairly based on your perception that they previously did the same to you. In situations like this, it can be important to at least consider the possibility that behaving fairly even when others have been unfair can contribute to making a better, fairer world for all.

Overuse of fairness

The overuse of fairness can manifest as trying to keep everyone in a family or work team perfectly happy. Striving toward that impossibility can lead to stress and tension. People can become obsessive trying to ensure that the exact amount of time spent with each child is the same or that no student gets what might be perceived by a few as special treatment. The reality is that different people have different needs and wants, and different beliefs about what would be fair, and that can make finding a solution that balances everyone's positions in a situation impossible. Sometimes, the best you can do is to try to be fair—to try to make your approach and the potential outcomes fair.

It is also possible for some people to become preoccupied with injustices committed against certain groups, or to surrender themselves to the goals of a larger group. It's important to monitor your fairness to yourself, to make sure you don't use up your personal resources for the good of others. If you give too much of yourself, your ability and willingness to fight for fairness for others can be compromised.

Avery J., 55, is a human resources manager who shares a story about the overuse of fairness:

Sometimes there just isn't a fair option. A few years ago my company had to downsize, and as a supervisor I had to decide who would go. There was no way I could make a fair decision—believe me, I tried and tried to think of every possible way to be fair. Everyone in my department was pulling their weight, doing their job. I started to wonder if I should do it based on personal needs, like who had more children, who was a single parent. How can you make the right choice when there isn't one? I really lost sleep over that one. I couldn't eat. I was really unhappy. I developed a physical condition. I even almost lost my job because of how long I delayed my decisions. My drive for fairness—my very best strength—was actually getting the best of me. In the end, I made the best choices I could, but I know some of the people I had to fire thought I was being unfair or playing favorites. That really hurt me.

Optimal use of fairness:
The golden mean

Fairness motto:

"I treat everyone equally and fairly, and give everyone the same chance by applying the same rules to everyone."

FAIRNESS

Imagine this:

Imagine that the optimal use of fairness is attempting to treat everyone equally while considering the individuality of each person and the uniqueness of each context in which decisions are made. You strive to give everyone a fair chance, applying the same general rules for everyone. See yourself at work and home examining how well you abide by principles of fairness, and doing what you can to consider fairness in each of your decisions that have implications for other people. Keep an eye out for opportunities to express fairness. Consider what you will do if a co-worker (or a family member) starts complaining that things aren't fair. How will you respond to them? What character strengths will you bring forth to respond (fairly) to their complaint? How might your strengths of teamwork, honesty, or leadership help you with your logical, justice-based reasoning? How might your strengths of forgiveness, love, and kindness help you with your care-based reasoning in this situation?

LEADERSHIP

WHAT WHY HOW

What to Know About Leadership

Leadership can take on many forms. As a character strength, leadership refers to the tendency to organize and encourage a group to get things done, while maintaining good relations within the group. Like teamwork, leadership involves being committed to the goals of the group, but how that commitment manifests itself is very different. Leadership involves setting goals and accomplishing them, enlisting effective help, building coalitions, and smoothing ruffled feathers. Effective leaders are able to provide a positive vision or message that inspires dedicated followers who feel empowered and perhaps even inspired.

The best leaders are self-aware. They recognize their top character strengths and how to use them to bring out the best in others. The VIA Survey does not limit leadership to what is sometimes referred to as "Big L" leadership, leadership typically displayed by presidents of corporations, politicians, and other movers and shakers. Its goal is to be sensitive to "small l" leadership, which is everyday leadership, sometimes informal, and is involved in directing and guiding any kind of group.

As someone high in leadership, you are able to build good group functioning, and to appreciate and empower the character strengths of those in your group, school, family, or company. You are good at organizing and planning group activities, while helping everyone feel included and important in the group experience. When you are at your best as a leader, you display good social awareness, and a high level of flexibility in approaching different personality styles. At times this may mean being directive and delegating, at other times inspiring, and at still other times being supportive.

WHAT   **WHY**   **HOW**

Why Leadership Is Valuable

Research findings on the benefits of the strength of leadership include the following:

- Socially, leaders are respected and valued by others, and they experience the benefits of being well-respected and held in high esteem by others.
- Leadership is related to emotional stability, openness, good social intelligence, and conscientiousness.
- Leaders are able to organize groups and achieve the goals of the group effectively.
- Good leaders bring out the best in others. Leadership allows you to use and express a number of key character strengths,

particularly zest, social intelligence, curiosity, creativity, prudence, honesty, and self-regulation.

How to Ignite Your Leadership

REFLECTING

Consider these questions as you reflect on your strength of leadership:

- How do you specifically express your strength of leadership?
- How do you feel when you're leading others?
- What is the difference between how effective you have been as a leader and how much you enjoy being a leader? How can you bring them into better agreement?
- How do your leadership tendencies become problematic?
- What have been your greatest leadership successes and challenges?
- What are the character strengths ingredients that are central to having people work together successfully toward a common goal or purpose?
- How do you decide when to lead and when to allow others to lead?
- How do people respond to your leadership?
- How do you keep the two key tasks of leadership—getting things done and helping people get along—in mind while you are leading?

Meet Rosita B., 62, a community organizer:

I remember when I was a kid, and we had to do group projects for school, I always found myself talking more than anyone else. Other people would be goofing off or not saying anything, but I'd be the one saying, "OK, how are we going to do this? Who's going to do what?" I'm not sure why that happened, but I think it helped that I was in a very small school all the way through high school. It was pretty much all the same kids the entire time, so we all fell into certain roles. At some point, it just seemed to become my job to organize things. I also think I was good at it: people listened to me, no one seemed to resent my doing it.

When I left work to become a full-time parent, I still fell into the same pattern. People were unhappy with some of the things going on in my kids' school, so I started going to the school board meetings, raising my voice, asking questions. A year later, I was asked to run for the school board, and then five years later I was the head of the school board. It just feels comfortable to me to lead, and others seem to feel comfortable with my leading. I feel like I flow when I'm running a meeting, getting everyone involved, moving the agenda along, but doing it in a way where I let everyone feel heard.

In relationships

- Organize a family event that brings together people who don't normally interact.
- Consider what needs to get done around your house. Negotiate and delegate a task to someone in your family while also taking

the lead on a task yourself. Try to make the task fit the best person for the job.

At work

- Organize a social event for some of your colleagues or a celebration for someone's birthday, anniversary, or workplace accomplishment. Take charge by organizing the people, setting, activities, and logistics.
- Lead an activity, assignment, or project and actively solicit opinions from group members.
- Consider key leadership role models—past and present—in your life. What behaviors did they display? What standards did they set? What leadership characteristics might be best to imitate?
- Discuss with someone who reports to you about how they can align their top character strength more in their work.

Within your community

- Gather and lead a group to help support a cause you believe in.
- Organize an event in the community that allows you to manage people and coordinate the experience from start to finish.
- Look for opportunities to practice taking a leadership role in activities, groups, and organizations, no matter how minor the responsibility.

Turned inward

- Lead yourself! Consider a personal issue, challenge, or weakness in which you are lagging in taking action. Activate your leadership to orchestrate an action plan. Be sure to savor the sense of accomplishment along the way.

FINDING BALANCE

Underuse of leadership

If you are identified as a leader ("positional leadership"), or find yourself in a situation where you should step up and lead ("situational leadership"), underuse occurs when you don't bring your strengths to the situation or you resist taking charge.

Leadership underuse can be seen in people who end up in leadership positions without personal motivation, and do not feel ready for or interested in the role. It can also be seen when people take on leadership roles because they are interested in leadership but don't think through how best to lead. In this situation, thinking about their strengths and the strengths of the people on the team can help them to create a more rewarding outcome for everyone. As leadership often involves a fair degree of effort and sustained energy, people high in leadership may find themselves feeling overwhelmed and pulling back when their active leadership is needed. When leaders forgo attention to their own strengths or the strengths of their followers, then they are almost certainly underusing their leadership strength.

Overuse of leadership

Too much leadership is controlling. This might come across as bossy or mean-spirited. Leadership overuse can be a collection of mismatches—a mismatch between personalities (leaders and subordinates), a mismatch between team members' strengths and their roles in the team, a mismatch between leadership style and the culture of the team, and so forth. Too much leadership can lead to disgruntled, rebellious, or subservient team members, none of which are optimal for a family, friendship group, team, school, or company.

Bob A., 42, is a small-business owner who has insights into his overuse of leadership:

As a leader, I have frequently gotten into conflicts with people. Sometimes I get lazy and just tell people what to do rather than really seeing what the best fit is for them. No doubt I come across as a bossy boss at times. Sometimes I have gotten frustrated and yelled at an employee or we get into a heated debate that is not a pleasant experience. But when I try to be a compassionate and supportive leader, the conflicts go way down. My problem is I can get stressed out with time pressures with our products, and I respond by getting fired up and angry. When that happens, I give no attention to how others think and feel and how they are working together. Instead, I seem to try to exert lots more control over the process, wanting things to be just the way I think they should be. I don't think people like that approach, so I'm trying to work on managing my stress in other ways.

Optimal use of leadership:
The golden mean

Leadership motto:
"I take charge and guide groups to meaningful goals, and ensure good relations among group members."

Imagine this:

Imagine you are a thoughtful, strengths-based leader. You lead small groups toward a productive result. You help to organize the process, troubleshoot issues, and contribute as well as lead. You value the relationships among the group members and try to ensure that everyone feels involved, appreciated for their contributions, and is willing to use their character strengths and talents. You are repeatedly grateful for your role as leader and the work of each member of the group. Strengths of fairness, kindness, and social intelligence are your closest companions. Take notice of how these strengths are expressed in your leadership.

VIRTUE OF TEMPERANCE

FORGIVENESS

HUMILITY

PRUDENCE

SELF-REGULATION

Strengths That Help You Manage Habits and Protect Against Excess

The virtue of temperance is, in some ways, the flip side of courage. Where courage involves your taking action when necessary to do good, temperance has to do with keeping yourself from acting in ways that are bad or socially undesirable. There are very different internal processes going on. At an emotional level, courage is mainly about anxiety and fear. It takes courage to act for good even when you are afraid or see risks in your potential actions. When you act temperately, the emotions you are fighting are more likely to be anger, laziness, or arrogance. These emotions can drive you to act in a way that damages others, a group, or the community. Where the courageous person is likely to be seen as a person of action, the temperate person more likely appears to others to be reserved, contemplative, and perhaps even tranquil. Just as it is inaccurate to consider a person courageous who acts because he or she doesn't experience fear when others would, it's not accurate to consider a person temperate who tends not to jump into action because they are more fearful than most people. In both cases, actions are being driven by uncontrolled emotions rather than by a recognition of what is the right thing to do.

Temperance encompasses four strengths, and the role of feelings in each can be spelled out. *Forgiveness* is a strength that requires overcoming feelings of anger, sadness, or fear caused by another person's transgressions against us. *Humility* often has to do with controlling our desire for attention from others, and letting our actions speak for themselves. *Prudence* is about avoiding impulsive tendencies, and waiting to act until risks can be effectively controlled. *Self-regulation* is about overcoming laziness to achieve our goals. Even though each strength is associated with certain types of actions, those actions each involve controlling certain types of emotions. You will notice in our descriptions of the temperance strengths that we sometimes discuss what a person with that strength does *not* do. It is this restraint or protective quality against excess, that characterizes the temperance strengths. Said simply, forgiveness protects us from hate, humility protects us from arrogance, prudence protects us from bad choices, and self-regulation protects us from an undisciplined life.

FORGIVENESS

WHAT **WHY** **HOW**

What to Know About Forgiveness

Forgiveness means to extend understanding toward those who have wronged or hurt us. It means to let go. In many cases this is the letting go of some or all of the frustration, disappointment, resentment, or other painful feelings associated with an offense. Forgiveness, and the related quality of mercy, involve accepting the shortcomings, flaws, and imperfections of others and giving them a second (or third) chance. As the expression goes, it is letting bygones be bygones, rather than being vengeful. It is a process of humanizing those who have led us to feel dehumanized.

Forgiveness is a powerful corrective against hatred. In many ways, forgiveness is a healing character strength, not only for the person forgiven but oftentimes even more so for the person doing the forgiving.

It's important to clarify that forgiveness does *not* mean forgetting the past or the harm caused to you. It does *not* mean you are condoning future bad behavior, or that you believe there should be no punishment for what was done to you. Equally important, forgiveness does *not* mean denying any pain you feel for what was done to you. Forgiveness also does *not* require reconciliation, the restoration of a broken relationship or feelings of trust. Forgiveness is more of a psychological response than a behavioral one, a response that involves rising above the hurt you feel to experience benevolence in a difficult situation. While forgiveness is primarily about your attitude toward the perpetrator, it can also become about your personal healing.

When you are at your best with forgiveness, you let go of resentment and negative judgments aimed at the person who has hurt you. You see the situation realistically, accurately assessing how much has been lost. You see the struggles and suffering—the humanity—of the offender, and you feel compassion for them.

WHAT　　　WHY　　　HOW

Why Forgiveness Is Valuable

Research findings on the benefits of the strength of forgiveness include the following:
- Apologies promote forgiveness.
- Partners who characterize their relationship as highly satisfying, committed, and close are more likely to forgive when transgressions occur.
- Forgiveness contributes to productive interpersonal relationships, thriving teamwork, job satisfaction, personal morale, innovative problem-solving, a sense of flexibility when facing changes, and productivity.

- More forgiving people experience less of the negative emotions of anger, anxiety, depression, and hostility than do less forgiving people.
- Forgiveness contributes to emotional stability and likability.
- Forgiveness is associated with physical and psychological health benefits such as emotional well-being, healthy lifestyle behaviors, social support, and a sense of spiritual well-being.

WHAT   **WHY**   **HOW**

How to Ignite Your Forgiveness

REFLECTING

Consider these questions as you reflect on your strength of forgiveness:

- What are the circumstances in which it is easy for you to be forgiving? Who is easiest to forgive in your life? Why?
- Are there situations in which you continue to withhold forgiveness?
- How does it feel when you forgive someone?
- How do you reconcile forgiving someone while holding the belief that people should be held accountable for transgressions?
- What are the advantages of forgiving someone, and what are the disadvantages?
- As you think about past situations, has it been more challenging to forgive someone at work or someone at home? Why?

SPOTTING THE STRENGTH

Meet Angelo M., 68, a retired maintenance worker:

One of my most central beliefs is the importance of forgiveness. What's amazing about it is that it's not just that I think it's the right thing to do. It has been a part of how I cope when I've been wronged by someone. One time my friend and I were mugged. We were lucky, there was a police officer passing by and they caught the guy who robbed us. My friend had a hard time getting over it. He was still very upset about the whole thing a year later, angry with the mugger for robbing him and for making him feel scared. But I figured it was my opportunity to practice forgiveness. I thought maybe he really needed the money and had no other options, but even if that wasn't true, I could still choose to forgive him. Once I realized that, I found I wasn't angry or upset about it. I didn't have to think about it anymore. I could move on.

TAKING ACTION

In relationships

- Forgiveness occurs when you allow yourself to move past the negative feelings that occur when others hurt or disappoint you and move forward to create positive experiences. Err toward talking things through with a family member or friend rather than cutting off communication or emotional ties. Think of transgressions in the context of your entire relationship. Consider how you might talk things through with someone important in your life as a pathway to forgiveness.

- Make a list of individuals against whom you hold a grudge. Choose one person either to meet with personally to discuss your grudge, or visualize a conversation in which you practice forgiveness and letting go.
- Forgiveness can be built by writing about the personal benefits that may have resulted from a negative incident. After a minor offense, write about the personal benefits that resulted.

At work

- Consider something small that recently offended you that your boss, subordinate, or colleague said or did. Reflect on their perspective—whether you agree with it or not—and practice letting go of resentment.
- If someone offends you at work, take time to think about how the person is a complex human being who needs to experience positive growth and transformation, rather than seeing them as "all bad."

Within your community

- Practice letting go of minor irritants in your life, such as someone cutting you off in traffic, or feeling slighted because someone ignored you or didn't consider your feelings.

Turned inward

- Practice self-forgiveness. Consider a minor wrongdoing and take the edge off your emotion by practicing forgiving yourself. Give yourself permission to have made the mistake while committing yourself to doing better in the future.

FINDING BALANCE

Underuse of forgiveness

Forgiveness can be underused when it competes with your sense of fairness. For example, when a person misbehaves, you can be angry that they didn't treat you fairly and feel they should be punished. Forgiveness can feel like letting the offender off too easily.

Other times, a person may withhold forgiveness as a self-protective measure. For example, forgiveness can leave you open to being hurt by that person again in the future, so forgiving the person can feel dangerous. You may restore a relationship with the transgressor and thereby feel vulnerable to subsequent hurt and disappointment. If instead you maintain an unforgiving and even hostile stance, then if there are subsequent offenses, you may feel better protected against that hurt. In this situation, it is useful to weigh the possible outcomes of many supportive character strengths such as perspective, judgment, kindness, and fairness, any of which may be provided by others who support you.

Forgiveness of yourself can also be underused. You may criticize yourself too much when you fail, showing a lack of self-compassion for your flaws and mistakes. The underuse of this strength, in any form, is a clear cause of mental (and sometimes even physical) suffering.

Overuse of forgiveness

When a person is highly forgiving of others, that person can become too permissive. As was the case with kindness, the overuse of this strength creates the possibility of being treated like a doormat.

Not every person and situation deserves a second, third, or fourth chance; each person and situation will dictate the optimal approach. Forgiving doesn't mean forgetting or giving up on expecting appropriate punishment. It's up to the forgiving person to account for not only the well-being of others but also the well-being of themselves.

Traci T., 57, a delivery person, had this to say about her overuse of forgiveness:

I think my ability to forgive people maybe has hurt me along the way. I've had some bosses who took advantage of me. They would give me things to do that they knew would make me stay late, or that weren't supposed to be part of my job. My friends tell me I'm a pushover. The same thing with my kids. Sometimes they were mean or oppositional to me growing up, always talking back to me, and my husband wanted me to be harder on them, but I would immediately forgive them. I always told myself I did this out of love and that they would become really forgiving people. It turns out they still expect me to quickly forgive them for their wrongdoings. They don't easily take responsibility for their actions. That has been disappointing for me.

Optimal use of forgiveness:
The golden mean

Forgiveness motto:
"I forgive others when they upset me and/or when they behave badly toward me, and I use that information in my future relations with them."

Imagine this:

Imagine you are interested in building your forgiveness strength. You start by focusing on the small things that irritate you, practicing the art of letting go. You let go of frustrations when you are in traffic and when people cut you off. Then, you turn to letting go of quirks and foibles of family and friends you love the most. Eventually, you find yourself ready to forgive someone for a larger offense. With each experience, you notice the emotions and positive effect of the letting go. You remind yourself that forgiving someone is a gift to them but can also be a gift to you.

To manage the overuse of forgiveness, you maintain perspective on the bigger picture, keeping your character strengths of fairness and love nearby in each situation, and closely considering the well-being of yourself and others within the broader scope of the situation.

HUMILITY

WHAT | **WHY** | **HOW**

What to Know About Humility

Humility means accurately evaluating your accomplishments. It's easy to describe what humility is not—it is not bragging, not doing things in excess, not seeking the spotlight, not drawing attention to yourself, not viewing yourself as more special or important than others. On the other hand, it is not bowing to every wish or demand of another person and it is not being highly self-critical. Truly humble people think well of themselves and have a good sense of who they are, but they also are aware of their mistakes, gaps in their knowledge, and imperfections. Most importantly, they are content without being a center of attention or getting praised for their accomplishments.

Modesty is an aspect of humility that is more external: doing things to lessen the attention on yourself, which is based on the choices you make, your appearance, and not embodying a "look at me" approach. Indeed, humble and modest people would rather blend into the crowd than stand out.

If you are high in humility, you are good at putting others first and giving them attention or letting them take the spotlight. In turn, this contributes to your being well-liked. The humble person finds it easy to make friends. Humility protects you from shifting into self-serving modes of arrogance or being driven by ego needs. When you're at your best with humility, you have a balanced and accurate view of yourself and see your place in the larger world, readily acknowledging your imperfections, and helping others to be successful.

WHAT　　**WHY**　　**HOW**

Why Humility Is Valuable

Research findings on the benefits of the strength of humility include the following:

- Humility is linked with good self-esteem and a positive self-view.
- Humble people are likely to demonstrate higher levels of gratitude, forgiveness, spirituality, and general health.
- Humility strengthens social bonds. In addition, research shows humble people are more helpful, agreeable, and generous.
- Other people typically like humble individuals and feel less threatened by them.
- The experience of emotional wellness, self-control, and feeling less self-preoccupied are additional benefits.
- Humility has been shown in studies to be associated with perseverance, self-regulation, and kindness toward others.
- Humility is also related to having less anxiety about death and to religious tolerance.

WHAT	WHY	HOW

HUMILITY

How to Ignite Your Humility

REFLECTING

Consider these questions as you reflect on your strength of humility:

- What are the advantages of being humble?
- How do others respond to your humility?
- Where does your humility come from and how do you express it?
- How does humility limit your life or get in your way?
- How do you balance humility with a need for recognition and appreciation?

SPOTTING THE STRENGTH

Meet Grace D., 60, a retired schoolteacher:

I never really thought of myself as a humble person until I took the VIA Survey, but now I finally see it in me. Maybe that's part of being humble, not knowing you are humble till someone points it out! A few times over the years I received awards as a teacher, such as the teacher of the year, those kinds of things. I would just say to myself, "Well, that's nice, but I was just doing my job." In fact, there were times I would do something that really pleased me—finished a drawing, or did something creative in my classroom. I was able to acknowledge my success with it, but I also enjoyed that no one else really knew about it. I knew then I was doing it just to please me.

Humility has certainly helped me in putting extra attention on my kids and spouse—all of whom have needed it quite a bit over the years—and I think that focus on them has helped each of them.

I see some people in my profession who are real blowhards. They let you know how great they are, what a good teacher they are, or the amazing things they've done. That always struck me as a little pathetic, like they need my attention or even do these special things just to get that attention. I trust someone more when I discover for myself the amazing things they're doing than if they tell me. I was an art history teacher, and I love modern art, but I was always uncomfortable with how some of the artists I taught would boast or do all sorts of flashy things to bring attention to themselves. I once came across this line from an art critic: "The first test of a great man is his humility." I think that doesn't just apply to art; it's the quiet person who does the greatest things, even if they don't get the most attention.

TAKING ACTION

In relationships

- Write a personal account of a time when you were especially humble, but not critical of yourself, in one of your relationships.
- Prime yourself to be humble before interacting in one of your close relationships. This means spending a few minutes thinking about humility and how you could act modestly with the person in an upcoming situation.

- Ask someone you trust to give you feedback on your struggles and areas of improvement.

At work

- Express humility by listening attentively to your co-workers' ideas, and compliment them when you feel they have good input without trying to add your ideas as well.
- Notice if you speak more than others in a group or team situation, and focus on the other people in the group.
- Think of a situation in which you focus much more on your needs, feelings, or interests than on those of others. In the next exchange, spend the majority of time focusing on the other person and their hopes, needs, views, and ideas.

Within your community

- Determine whether you are less modest around certain groups of people, and if so, try a different approach.
- Look for exemplars of humility/modesty in your community. Reflect on the evidence that supports their humility. Communicate your findings with others.

Turned inward

- Take time to observe and appreciate your many character strengths, talents, interests, and resources by "sitting with" these strengths (perhaps literally sitting in a quiet space) and appreciating them in a positive, upbeat, balanced and completely humble way.

FINDING BALANCE

Underuse of humility

To brag and portray yourself as better or more important than others is to underuse humility. In some cultures, boasting is actively punished. The relative infrequency of humility across the globe as a signature strength, and the relatively lower relationship between humility and other character strengths, suggests it may be common to underuse humility in many cultures. Bragging about your accomplishments can be an important part of achieving success in certain fields. What represents underuse of humility therefore has to be considered in light of your culture's expectations.

Most people want to share their successes and accomplishments—at least to a small degree—with others because it feels good to feel appreciated. Moreover, the sharing of good events has been shown to benefit well-being for the speaker and listener. In other words, it's normal and healthy to share your character strength stories, positive experiences that took place during the day, and positive contributions or accomplishments. The underuse of humility emerges, however, when you take this to a level of boasting, when the sole focus or purpose is to promote yourself, or when you are conveying you are "the kindest person" or the "most fair-minded at work."

Each of us has ego needs that vary over time, and all of us seek recognition or approval from time to time. Thus, even people high in humility can find themselves being uncharacteristically self-promoting in certain situations. Underuse can unwittingly occur when you don't consider how much others have contributed to your own success; or when you discount someone who is receiving an accolade because you did not receive one as well; or when you are unable to set aside competitiveness to appreciate another person's accomplishment.

Overuse of humility

The overuse of humility turns into something else—self-deprecation, excessive self-criticism, or subservience. Although a reasonable level of humility is associated with good self-esteem, an excessive degree of humility can be indicative of poor self-image. A subtle reality of humility overuse is that the humble person is denying themselves to other people who may want to get to know more about them. This can obstruct relationships from developing, because people don't get the opportunity to know you, or they may even think you are secretive or withholding about yourself. Some forms of humility overuse reflect an unhealthy degree of skepticism or negativity about yourself.

Sachihiro M., 30, is a radiology technician who has experiences with the overuse of humility:

I view myself as a humble and modest person. I never brag about anything and I don't talk much about myself. I ask other people questions and just try to have fun in life. I'm happy with my job and my current relationship. I don't try especially hard to have or be "the best" of anything. I'm content with the status quo. When I see others push themselves to advance at their job or to keep improving their relationship, I question whether I should do more, push for more achievements, and talk my way "up the ladder" at work.

I'm a very private person. Very few people know me other than superficialities. I don't share much about myself, my problems, or the good things I do in my community. I can see where this limits me when I'm meeting new people because they don't get to know who I really am. They don't know some of the big things I've overcome in my life. Then, I see others sharing that kind of thing and it inspires people. I could probably inspire people, too, with my stories, but I just don't tend to go there.

HUMILITY

Optimal use of humility:
The golden mean

Humility motto:
"I see my strengths and talents but I am humble, not seeking to be the center of attention or to receive recognition."

Imagine this:

Imagine yourself expressing humility across the main domains of your life. Is there one domain where you are less humble than others; for example, at work or in community organizations? Increase your use of humility in that domain. View yourself as attending to various people in that domain, lifting them up, and celebrating their work. You can use your prudence strength to plan how you can use humility in this way.

You are aware of your character strengths and you express them in your life. In other words, you are honest with yourself—you know who you are and aren't afraid to show it. You share your successes, accomplishments, and positive events of your day but you don't dwell on them, you don't embellish them, and you don't believe you are more special than anyone else because of them.

You see the value of the human condition and your place and others' place in the grander scheme of not only work and family, but life.

PRUDENCE

WHAT | WHY | HOW

What to Know About Prudence

Prudence means being careful about your choices, stopping and thinking before acting. It is a strength of restraint. When you are prudent, you are not taking unnecessary risks, and not saying or doing things that you might later regret. If you are high in prudence, you are able to consider the long-term consequences of your actions. Prudence is a form of practical reasoning, the ability to examine the potential consequences of your actions objectively, and to control yourself based on that examination.

You might view prudence as "wise caution." Prudence involves being careful with your choices and good in your decision-making. Those who are prudent can certainly take risks and be spontaneous, but they will weigh the pros and cons of their actions, think things through prior to acting, and continue that process as more information becomes available. When you are at your best with prudence, you plan and are careful, looking at the bigger picture and taking reasonable risks that lead to growth and goal progress.

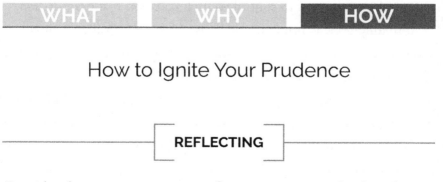

Why Prudence Is Valuable

Research findings on the benefits of the strength of prudence include the following:

- Prudence is associated with intelligence and optimism.
- Prudence is associated with better physical health, job performance, and student achievement.
- Prudence helps us to avoid the mishaps of life, both physical and psychological.
- Prudence is associated with cooperativeness, assertiveness, interpersonal warmth, and insightfulness.
- Prudence is associated with productivity and the ability to be conscientious, most likely because the prudent person tends not to enter into agreements unless he or she believes there is a good chance of a successful outcome.

How to Ignite Your Prudence

REFLECTING

Consider these questions as you reflect on your strength of prudence:

- What are the personal benefits you experience in being prudent?
- How has prudence served you well over the years, in big and small ways?
- In what areas of life are you most prudent and least prudent?
- How do other people respond to your prudence?
- What regrets do you have about times you held yourself back from taking a risk?

PRUDENCE

SPOTTING THE STRENGTH

Meet Jan F., 38, a middle management executive:

I've always been a reserved person. My friends in high school would do crazy things, and I was always careful about it. Maybe I was just less of a risk-taker than some of them, but I didn't really get the pleasure in doing something just because of a risk of getting hurt. That's continued in my adult life. I have taken risks in my career, but I take "measured risks" that I know have a good chance of paying off. It doesn't always happen, but I like to play the odds. For example, I never play the lottery, and I don't like to gamble, because why would I bet in a situation where I know the odds are stacked against me? I'd rather volunteer for a project at work that I know has the possibility to succeed, and if it does, it's going to improve my reputation in the company and their desire to keep me in the future.

I see the idea of thinking about the odds of success as an important part of prudence. Over the years I've become known as someone you can come to for advice, and I'll say to people, "What are the odds that's going to work out for you?" and sometimes it's like people have never thought of their decisions in those terms before. A lot of people just look at the possible prize and don't think about their chances of getting that prize or how much work would be involved in getting it, and I think they make bad decisions because of it.

TAKING ACTION

In relationships

- Consult with a trusted friend or significant other to get his or her view before taking on another project or assignment.

- In one of your closest relationships, practice pausing to think and reflect before each thing you say. Notice the effects throughout the week.

- Examine an event from the past when you used prudence to the benefit of a close relationship.

At work

- When you organize and plan things before you act so that you minimize the risk of making mistakes or falling short of goals, then you are exercising prudence. Take time to make a plan before starting a task, so you can keep the details as well as the long-term goals in mind as you work.

- Conduct a cost-benefit analysis when facing difficult or risky situations at work: What are the benefits of doing "x"? What are the costs of doing "x"? What are the benefits of *not* doing "x"? What are the costs of *not* doing "x"?

- Remove all extraneous distractions before you make your next three important decisions on a work project.

- Before you make a decision that is typically very easy, take one full minute to think about it before you take action.

Within your community

- If your community is involved in a heated debate, attend a meeting and see if you can be a voice of prudence. Wait until both sides have said their piece before speaking, and see if you can come up with a possible compromise that would be acceptable to both.
- Drive cautiously; notice your mental activity and bodily sensations as you do so. Remind yourself that there are fewer time-sensitive emergencies than you think.

Turned inward

- Write down your plans for each hour of the remainder of the day, no matter how trivial. Consider your thoughts, motivations, desires, and emotions about each plan.

FINDING BALANCE

Underuse of prudence

In today's quick-fix, quick-action, social media culture, we can feel compelled to respond quickly rather than thinking before we act (or type). Prudence underuse is common. Short attention spans for anything other than the excessive, the extraordinary, the colorful, or the exciting contribute to this phenomenon.

Although being prudent is generally comforting to people high in this character strength, it can at times cause them to feel bad about their lack of spontaneity, and they may feel pressure from others to throw caution to the wind. Thus, prudent people can find themselves swing-

PRUDENCE

ing to the other extreme of being imprudent. For example, a prudent person may purposely decide to approach a vacation in a spontaneous fashion instead of following his or her impulses to plan every detail. This may work out fine, but can result in less desirable outcomes.

Overuse of prudence

Sometimes others can perceive prudence negatively, as stuffiness, inhibition, rigidity, or passivity. However, this is not the balanced, healthy expression of prudence: these are descriptors of the overuse of prudence! If someone is repeatedly refusing to challenge themselves or move out of their comfort zone, then prudence overuse might be at play. Prudence overuse is sometimes associated with anxiety about uncertainty. Too much prudence and caution can limit the development of relationships, stymie self-improvement, or minimize career opportunities.

Bill T., 58, is a financial planner who offers some insights into his overuse of prudence:

> I know I've passed up opportunities that would have paid off for me because I was scared to take the risk. And in some of those cases, such as taking on a bit more work, I could have done it. I had a particular way that I did things, and I didn't want to risk changing my routine. It took me a while to meet my wife because I was very limited in how I went about meeting new people. When I did meet people, I sometimes came across as a bit stuffy or as having an "air" about me. There have been many instances where I've thrown caution to the wind and just went for it. Those often do pan out well for me, but it's just not my personality to act like that a lot of the time. Certainly, prudence has served me well overall in my job as a financial planner, and I make good investments for my family and clients. But even with that I can find examples where I

got too rigid with keeping one type of very secure portfolio, which led me to not go down a different path that would have brought in more money.

Optimal use of prudence:
The golden mean

Prudence motto:

"I act carefully and cautiously, looking to avoid unnecessary risks and planning with the future in mind."

Imagine this:

Imagine you are bringing prudence to your life in an optimal way. You are on time, respectful, and carefully plan your day and your week. You plan many of your work tasks using self-regulation and discipline, and you set up some fun activities for your family on the evenings and weekends. When challenges arise, you pause to think things through rather than reacting impulsively. You use your judgment to look at the details of problems and use honesty as you share your solutions and plans with others.

You begin to see the safe havens in life where you can feel comfortable being less cautious. You see where there is a time to be brave and a time to be prudent, and a time for using both strengths at once.

SELF-REGULATION

WHAT   WHY   HOW

What to Know About Self-Regulation

Self-regulation is a complex character strength. It has to do with controlling your appetites and emotions, and regulating what you do. Those high in self-regulation have a good level of confidence in their belief that they can be effective in what they pursue and are likely to achieve their goals. They are admired for their ability to control their reactions to disappointment and insecurities. Self-regulation helps keep a sense of balance, order, and progress in life.

The mantra of the self-regulated person is that you know when "enough is enough." When you are at your best with self-regulation, you exercise discipline and self-control with your health habits, emotions, and impulses, while allowing yourself spontaneous pleasures and staying reasonably flexible in your daily routines.

A central element of self-regulation is being disciplined. It means to make measured decisions about what you eat, drink, and generally consume, as well as your activity level. This does not imply perfect regulation, but a self-regulated person has a highly developed sense of control in managing these behaviors, pursuing their goals, and living up to certain standards.

Self-regulation can take many forms. In addition to managing your habits, behaviors, impulses, and emotions, you can manage your attention. The self-regulation of attention is popularly known as mindfulness in which the person practicing mindfulness takes (some) control of what they place their attention on, whether that be their breathing, a candle flame, a loved one's smile, a bite of food, or the movement of their body while walking. In these examples of mindfulness, no person uses self-regulation to chronically stay in the present moment, rather the task is to continue *returning* to the present moment (which requires the strength of self-regulation).

The enemy of self-regulation is something called *delay discounting*. This occurs when the person gives up a better long-term outcome for one that is more immediate. If the long-term result is more desirable than the short-term one, the person high in self-regulation will focus on the long-term outcome. When you are at your best with self-regulation, you try your best to be disciplined with your health habits around eating, drinking, sleeping, and exercise, and you're able to keep your emotions and impulses in check in various situations. As this is done imperfectly, you apply self-compassion and self-forgiveness when your self-regulation wavers far away.

WHAT   WHY   HOW

Why Self-Regulation Is Valuable

Research findings on the benefits of the strength of self-regulation include the following:

- Children who are most successful at delaying gratification early in life are more successful academically and socially, and that success is long-lasting.
- People with high self-control report fewer symptoms of anxiety and depression, are better able to control anger, and generally get along better with people.
- People skilled at self-regulation are in charge of their emotions rather than the other way around.
- Self-regulation is associated with achieving goals and being successful in many endeavors, including academic, athletic, and work performance.
- Self-regulation is linked with better personal adjustment, such as having fewer physical and psychological problems and having a greater sense of self-acceptance and self-esteem in relationships.
- Self-control helps in the prevention and management of addictions.

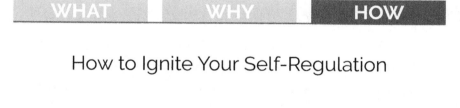

How to Ignite Your Self-Regulation

Consider these questions as you reflect on your strength of self-regulation:

- How does self-regulation play a role in your greatest successes in life?

- What areas of your life are best regulated?
- How do you control your unwanted impulses? What techniques or strategies do you use?
- Which areas of life or what circumstances are most challenging for you in terms of regulating emotions and impulses?
- What thoughts and feelings do you have about yourself when you are not self-regulating effectively?
- How do other people (friends, family, co-workers, or acquaintances) respond to your self-regulation?
- What areas of your life would be improved if you applied greater self-regulation?
- How does self-regulation affect your tolerance for situations that are vague or unpredictable?

SPOTTING THE STRENGTH

Meet Ethan E., 63, a retired business owner:

There are a lot of people that are more disciplined than me, but I have definitely set up some pretty good habits in my life. After my father died at a young age, I became concerned about my own health and being around long enough to see my three kids grow up. So I decided to get into shape. I started going to the gym every day, even if it meant getting up at 6 a.m., cut down on my drinking, and ate more health foods.

I became concerned about environmental issues, so I founded an organization in my community to work on those issues, and we've been very successful in getting new initiatives going in our town. I think it's really important when you set your mind to something that you are disciplined and focused to make it happen. Sometimes I've had to sacrifice other things I've wanted to do in the moment, but I've then seen the benefits come in the long term. This way of thinking has allowed me at this point to look back and feel good about what I've accomplished.

TAKING ACTION

In relationships

- Think of something you would like to change in your family that is likely to take some time and discipline, such as achieving more financial independence. Sit down and write out steps to achieve that goal and the obstacles you'll need to overcome. Set a time frame for each step. Use your self-control to implement this approach for (or with) your family.
- Try a new approach to sticking with an exercise or walking routine, and involve one of your close relationships in the discipline.
- The next time you feel angry in one of your relationships, step away and take a cooling-off period. Investigate the emotion you are feeling. Is hurt, sadness, or anxiety driving your anger? Decide whether to gently share your feelings or to engage in an activity that would be caring toward yourself (e.g., taking a warm bath).

At work

- Self-regulation at work expresses itself when you are able to manage emotions and impulses that might interfere with your own performance or the performance of others. A first step to controlling your emotions is to be aware of them as they arise when you are working on a project or talking with a colleague.

SELF-REGULATION

- Think of a long-term goal to achieve at work. Exert your self-control by following steps described earlier to reach your goal.
- Take notice of your posture throughout the day. When you notice yourself slouching, sitting uncomfortably, or displaying poor posture, balance yourself by straightening up. You might have to practice this several times each day to make this more conscious.

Within your community

- Make a to-do list for a neighborhood or community-oriented event, come up with an action plan, and begin to carry it out.

Turned inward

- Turn your self-regulation inward by taking control of your attention. As noted earlier, this is the practice of mindfulness meditation. Bring your attention to yourself—your thoughts, body sensations, emotions, motivations, and actions. Observe the changes in each of these elements, and keep an open awareness that does not get caught up in any one element, even if you experience something negative.
- Organize your daily life more effectively. Think of a better way to organize your kitchen, or your morning preparations for the day. Apply that organizing principle to larger and larger issues.

FINDING BALANCE

Underuse of self-regulation

The underuse of self-regulation is an important issue, as chronic underuse is central to a large number of the personal and social problems that plague people. That said, our lives would be havoc and our communities chaotic without a good deal of self-regulation. Even if we are low in self-regulation, we have more of this strength capacity than we realize, and our underuse or use of the strength can vary widely based on the situation. For example, you might manage your emotions and impulses beautifully during an eight-hour workday and then underuse self-regulation by overeating.

Self-regulation is a capacity that acts like a muscle—it can be fatigued by overexertion (and therefore be underused) in as few as seven minutes. It is also like a muscle in that it can be strengthened with practice. Self-regulation can certainly be underused in one particular domain. Many people underuse self-regulation of one or more of the following: sexual desires, finances, eating, drinking, working, exercising, focusing their attention (wandering thoughts), emotions, impulses/reactivity, and body posture, to name some of the most important. If you underuse in one area but not others, you can study the areas you are strong in to better understand your self-regulation habits. In other words, how is it that I self-regulate so well with my financial management and my exercise habits? How might my habits or methods of self-management with these be brought to bear to improve the domains where I am underusing?

Overuse of self-regulation

A person who overuses their self-regulation in a particular situation is referred to as being overcontrolled. They are overmanaging themselves in a rigid and sometimes detrimental way, sometimes controlling every morsel of food or drink, every minute of exercise, and stifling every hint of negative emotion. They might be described as inhibited or constricted, and even feel as though they are tightly wound, which is all part of their overcontrol. The overuse can become obsessive in terms of routine and behavior and wreak havoc on their relationships. In some cases, they may come across as acting superior, but in reality they are often deeply suffering.

Robyn P., 28, is a playwright and actress, who shares her story about the overuse of self-regulation:

As an actress for the stage I wanted to not only portray my characters, I wanted to embody them. For any new role, or any new audition, my disciplined self just takes over. I would often portray a fit or slender woman, and I would spend every waking moment managing my eating and exercising.

I remember for this one part, I was obsessive. It's not that all I did was exercise, it's that it occupied my mind all day. I was highly disciplined, doing various types of exercise multiple times per day and eating an exact, planned-out set of meals each day. I didn't deviate from these plans for months. I didn't go out to eat with my friends or family. I didn't so much as grab a snack at a coffee shop. Sure, I was eating healthy—and eating enough food—but it was very rigid and controlled. Part of me liked this discipline because I knew what to expect, I knew what my goals were, and I was successful. But part of me disliked it because I couldn't maintain any intimate relationships at the time, and I felt a loss of freedom. Also, I was pretty high-strung and stressed during those months, which affected my relationships with my family too. After my role was over, it was hard to break my habits. It took many months after that before I got things back to normal.

Optimal use of self-regulation:
The golden mean

Self-regulation motto:

"I manage my feelings and actions and am
disciplined and self-controlled."

Imagine this:

Imagine you are "in the zone" with your self-regulation. You have found the right balance for your life. You are managing your emotions, your exercise routine, your eating habits, and even your attention levels (meaning you're controlling your ability to focus and improve your attention). While it is impossible to be perfectly self-regulated in every situation, picture optimal use for you at this point in your life. What is balanced and self-regulated eating? Exercising? Emotional expression and control? Attentional focus? Take time to picture each of these areas and get a sense for how you can accomplish a healthy balance with each.

It will also be interesting to make note of the character strengths that will best support you. Zest to keep your energy up? Hope to picture this optimal use in the future clearly? Prudence and perseverance to help you plan for any goals and overcome obstacles as you take action?

VIRTUE OF TRANSCENDENCE

APPRECIATION OF BEAUTY & EXCELLENCE

GRATITUDE

HOPE

HUMOR

SPIRITUALITY

Strengths That Help You Connect to the Larger Universe and Provide Meaning

The last set of strengths involve the virtue of transcendence. Just as courage and temperance can be thought of as a matched set having to do with acting and restraining, and humanity and justice have to do with relationships with individuals and groups, transcendence can be contrasted with wisdom. Wisdom has to do with gaining knowledge, and using that knowledge to achieve good for yourself and others. The transcendent strengths have to do with our knowing there are things that we can never know or understand fully. They have to do with recognizing the limitations of our knowledge and using that recognition in the service of the good.

This description sounds a little abstract, we know, and transcendence is the most abstract of the virtues. Another way to think about transcendence is in comparison to humanity and justice. Where those two virtues involve looking outside ourselves to other people, transcendence has to do with looking outside ourselves to the basic nature of the world, the future, and even beyond the physical. The strengths that are associated with transcendence help us separate ourselves from our everyday lives and see into a larger way of thinking. Transcendence is often associated with the concept of the divine, whatever that may mean to you as a person. The strengths included in transcendence include *appreciation of beauty and excellence, gratitude, hope, humor,* and *spirituality*.

APPRECIATION OF BEAUTY AND EXCELLENCE

WHAT **WHY** **HOW**

What to Know About Appreciation of Beauty and Excellence

At the core of this character strength is the ability to see something delightful and moving in situations, environments, or other people, a special something that others may ignore. Appreciation of beauty and excellence involves noticing and appreciating beauty, uniqueness, virtue, skill, and the exceptional in everyday life. At its best, this strength emerges across domains, from nature and art, to mathematics and science, to human interactions.

To be more specific about it, there are at least three very different contexts in which this character strength tends to emerge:

1) The appreciation of natural beauty, such as sunsets or a view of light shimmering on a peaceful lake. These experiences tend to produce emotions of awe and wonder.

2) The appreciation of skill, talent, and other forms of excellence, such as an Olympic performance or a woodworker crafting an

impeccable piece of furniture. These experiences tend to produce feelings of admiration.

3) The appreciation of virtue and goodness in others, such as the display of forgiveness, kindness, fairness, or compassion. These experiences tend to produce feelings of elevation, which, in turn, inspire us to be good or kind to others as well.

Appreciation of beauty takes the form of seeing beauty in the small places such as one leaf on a tree, one glance outside, or the curling up of a person's lips to form a smile. Appreciation of excellence can also occur in a glance as you admire the architecture of a building or read a well-crafted book. In other words, this strength is about not taking things for granted; it is about valuing what is distinctive and special. When you are at your best with appreciation of beauty and excellence, you not only experience nature, art, literature, science, sports, music, movies, exceptional performance, and virtuous behaviors for their entertainment value; you also appreciate them for the way they elevate the human experience. In turn, you tend to want to improve yourself and be kinder to others.

WHAT   WHY   HOW

Why Appreciation of Beauty and Excellence Is Valuable

Research findings on the benefits of the strength of appreciation of beauty and excellence include the following:

- Appreciation of beauty and excellence is a strength that may help people in coping with emotional challenges or other difficulties. People who have experienced loss or suffering often find their appreciation of beauty is enhanced.

- The expression of this strength leads immediately to a positive emotional experience that can be identified as awe, admiration, or elevation, all of which contribute to feelings of well-being.
- This sense of awe and elevation when in the presence of great beauty or excellence heightens spirituality, sense of meaning, and the desire to be a better person.
- Appreciation of beauty and excellence is associated with a variety of health behaviors.
- Exercises focused on increasing the appreciation of beauty have been shown to boost happiness and lower depression, at least in the short term.

WHAT   WHY   HOW

How to Ignite Your Appreciation of Beauty and Excellence

REFLECTING

Consider these questions as you reflect on your strength of appreciation of beauty and excellence:

- Under what conditions (people, places, activities) are you most appreciative of beauty and excellence?

- How does appreciation of beauty or appreciation of excellence affect your work, relationships, use of leisure time, and community involvement?

- How have you nurtured your appreciation of beauty and excellence?

- To what extent do you appreciate beauty versus appreciate excellence?

- Does an appreciation of beauty or excellence ever overwhelm you in a positive or negative way? For example, a person can become overwhelmed by awe or the admiration of others, or a person can have such high standards of excellence that they struggle to measure up.

- How might you notice more moral beauty in your life, where you attend more closely to the goodness and virtuous behavior of others?

SPOTTING THE STRENGTH

Meet Bai R., 40, an interior designer:

I don't know much about perception and how information goes into brains, but I definitely perceive things visually first. From my earliest memory, I was like that. As a child, I was drawn to picture books with pictures of treasures, and the gold was like a shiny meal. It was like candy in a way. When I looked at those pictures, I felt excitement and pure joy.

It's the emotional part that matters to me; it's the joy that comes from it that matters. To me there's clearly a connection between appreciation of beauty and how information enters me and gets processed. Beautiful things, visually striking things, nourish me, like food. I am surprised when I find that people around me don't appreciate things the way I do. It feels as though they are almost blind to what is in front of them. I am compelled to point things out, and I am sometimes disappointed by the response I get.

I think my interest in beautiful things goes pretty deep. In my case, I'm driving my life both to create beauty and to eradicate ugliness. If I can replace a plastic lamp with a beautiful one, I think that whole process is productive and gives back to the people I work with. I don't think of it as an altruistic act necessarily, but it's a positive force. It's not just for me, but it's for everybody and anybody.

TAKING ACTION

In relationships

- Share your appreciation of beauty or excellence with one of your close relationships by listening to a piece of music or by watching a meaningful film and experiencing the positive emotions together.
- Keep a weekly log of moments in any of your relationships in which you feel inspired by the good acts you witness.

At work

- There are various strengths that contribute to working well, such as perseverance and self-regulation. When you do good work because you care about the beauty of things done well, your success at work may have more to do with your appreciation of excellence and beauty. Use this strength by noticing and supporting good ideas and elegant solutions.
- On a break at work, step away from your desk and either walk outside or look out a window and savor the beauty that you see. See if it revitalizes you for the work ahead.
- Arrange your work environment in a way that you find aesthetically pleasing, and make changes periodically.

- Spot the excellence of others. Be the voice of strengths recognition for those in your work life.

Within your community

- Notice and spend a moment observing at least one instance of natural beauty in your community every day.
- Take time to find out about the extraordinary efforts and skills of others in your neighborhood or city. Marvel at what they have accomplished in their past and share the positives with others in your community or communicate your positive feelings to the person directly.

Turned inward

- Pause to appreciate your inner beauty. One way to do this is to see your character strengths and recall how you have used them to bring benefit to others.

FINDING BALANCE

Underuse of appreciation of beauty and excellence

When we are caught up in our daily routines and stressors, it is easy to lose sight of what is happening in the present moment. The present moment is where we connect with beauty and excellence, whether it be an experience in nature, an impressive athletic performance, or an act of kindness by someone. Even those high in appreciation of beauty and excellence will underuse it in certain situations and miss opportunities to find beauty in what can seem mundane or routine, such as work, long-term relationships, familiar surroundings, and even themselves.

Overuse of appreciation of beauty and excellence

A keen appreciation of beauty and of excellence, when excessive, can result in perfectionism, snobbishness, and intolerance of others who don't share this appreciation. You may take offense when others threaten or disregard natural beauty, which may lead to an overuse in your taking an extreme position. Being too critical or demanding of excellence in certain situations can be an overuse if it negatively affects others. Some may not appreciate their own personal achievements because of highly perfectionistic standards, driven by a belief that "it's never good enough."

Brady L., 30, is a geologist who shares about the overuse of appreciation of beauty and excellence:

For my family, definitely, I think my drivenness toward beauty annoys them. I have a very specific idea about how things should look. My father once got an easy chair that just didn't go with the rest of the décor in my parents' living room. It drove me nuts. I let them know how I felt, and they were just amused by it. Finally, I showed up one day with a new chair, and took the previous one they had and gave it to the Salvation Army. My father looked at the chair I'd brought, and he smiled and said, "Yeah, that looks much better, but is it as comfortable?" It was. It's not that he doesn't have any taste; it's just that it doesn't matter that much to him. To me, though, at this point in my life, I just can't put up with anything less than beautiful. I know it can bother people though.

I also think sometimes I'm too impressed by people who have exquisite taste. Sometimes those aren't the nicest people. I've had a couple of relationships now with people who just impressed the hell out of me with their aesthetic sense, but our relationships were a disaster. As I've gotten older I've realized that the appreciation of beauty is nowhere near the most important thing in a relationship. My current partner has really good taste, but is also caring and really into me. It took me a long time to realize that that was more important than fashion sense.

Optimal use of appreciation of beauty and excellence: *The golden mean*

Appreciation of beauty and excellence motto:

"I recognize, emotionally experience, and appreciate the beauty around me and the skill of others."

Imagine this:

Imagine the first bite of your favorite dish. Notice the changing vibrant colors of fall leaves. See the forgiveness one friend gives to another friend. Observe the smooth and suave skill of a professional tennis player who appears to glide across the court. Savor each of these experiences, feel the feelings associated with them. Be grateful to be experiencing each one.

Now, imagine the first bite of a simple lunch and appreciate the flavors and tastes released. Observe one tree branch, root, flower, or leaf and see the fullness of life in it. Notice the good feelings in seeing someone give a donation to support a good cause. See the excellence in a child learning to play baseball and slowly building his or her skill.

Make note that in any moment of your day, you can turn your attention to appreciate the beauty, excellence, and goodness all around you.

GRATITUDE

WHAT   **WHY**   **HOW**

What to Know About Gratitude

The character strength of gratitude involves feeling and expressing a deep sense of thankfulness in life, and more specifically, taking the time to genuinely express thankfulness to others. This thankfulness can be for specific gifts or thoughtful acts. It could also more generally reflect recognition of what that person contributes to your life. We can be grateful for deliberate acts by others, such as a piece of art from a child, or for spontaneous treasures, such as a cool breeze on your face on a hot day. What marks gratitude is the psychological response: the transcendent feeling of thankfulness, the sense of having been given a gift by that person or event. Grateful people experience a variety of positive emotions, and those emotions inspire them to act in more virtuous ways—humbler, more persistent, or kinder. Gratitude tends to foster the character strengths of kindness and love, and therefore is closely associated with empathy and with connection to others.

There are three main components of gratitude: (a) a warm sense of appreciation for somebody or something, (b) a sense of good will toward that person or thing, and (c) a disposition to act positively that flows from that appreciation and good will. Gratitude typically makes people more open to experience and more agreeable.

When you are at your best with gratitude, you feel grateful for the positive things in your life, and you express thankfulness directly to others and often. You count your blessings regularly and reflect positively on how you have lived your life. Your gratitude opens the door to the use of other character strengths, such as kindness, curiosity, hope, spirituality, and zest.

WHAT **WHY** **HOW**

Why Gratitude Is Valuable

Research findings on the benefits of the strength of gratitude include the following:

- Gratitude is one of the strengths most connected to the experience of a meaningful life.
- Gratitude contributes to physical and psychological health, such as better cardiovascular and immune system functioning.
- Gratitude is one of the five strengths most robustly linked to satisfaction and happiness.
- Grateful people have better exercise habits, positive moods, and sleep patterns. They are less likely to be depressed, and more likely to engage in a wide range of behaviors aimed at helping others.
- Grateful people tend to have greater goal achievement, optimism, work enjoyment, and work calling. Among students, gratitude is associated with better grades.

- Gratitude has spiritual benefits as well, such as a feeling of inter-connectedness with life, a general sense of responsibility toward others, and reduced emphasis on material goods.
- Gratitude activities have been widely successful in boosting well-being and managing depression.

WHAT   **WHY**   **HOW**

GRATITUDE

How to Ignite Your Gratitude

REFLECTING

Consider these questions as you reflect on your strength of gratitude:

- What circumstances make it most likely you will experience gratitude? What circumstances make it most likely you will express gratitude?
- What is most rewarding to you about expressing gratitude? Is it more rewarding with certain people?
- Are there people to whom you have not adequately expressed gratitude, as an oversight or intentionally holding it back (e.g., family, friends, co-workers, mentors, community members)? If so, why?
- What concerns do you have, if any, in expressing gratitude to certain people?
- If someone does not express gratitude, does it make it less likely you will express gratitude toward them?
- What effect does it have on other people when you express gratitude?

- To what degree do you express gratitude to others out of a deep feeling of appreciation as opposed to social convention?

SPOTTING THE STRENGTH

Meet Gabriela G., 48, a librarian:

Developing an attitude of gratitude was a conscious, specific decision on my part. I was in the middle of my divorce, my kids were two and six, I had a full-time job and a house, lots of emotional and financial concerns, everything looked really bleak, and I was grasping for something to hold on to. Everything was up in the air. I remember driving home from work. I turned up my street and there was a magnificent sunset, and in that moment I went "Oh" and realized it was the brightest spot of my day. I felt a spiritual uplift, and I remember thinking, "This is what I need. I need more of this feeling," and thinking "How do I get that?" What I realized I was experiencing then was gratitude, that no matter how bad things got, I still had a lot in my life worth valuing and being grateful for. Realizing that took a weight off my shoulders.

Sometimes it feels like a game I play—my boyfriend came home and talked about someone in a much worse situation, and I'm grateful for my own circumstance. Other times, it's an exercise you have to do when you get mired in your stuff and have to get out of it. For me, especially, it's a defined skill; it's something I have to work on, like my physical exercises. You have to make a decision to do it and you have to look in every nook and cranny in your life. The times gratitude is most useful are the times it's hardest to find.

TAKING ACTION

In relationships

- Point out one small attribute or behavior of one of your close relationships that you appreciate but that typically goes unnoticed. Notice it and share it verbally with them.
- At the end of each day, make note of one good thing that happened in one of your relationships, however small, and why it happened.

At work

- Gratitude expresses itself at work when you let others know when you feel grateful for the opportunities your job affords you, or appreciate others for who they are or what they do. Share your appreciation on a Post-It Note that you put on someone's desk as a surprise or send it in a spontaneous email.
- Make a point to go out of your way to express thanks to someone at work who is not typically recognized. Be sure to offer a few sentences of explanation about why you are grateful to them and note the impact their actions have had on you.
- Write down three good things that happened at work and then reflect on why these good things have happened.

Within your community

- Express gratitude by leaving a note on the car or front door of someone who has offered you help in the past or whom you've noticed has done good things for your community.
- Thank a service worker in your community for their efforts over time; for example, a bus driver, a store clerk, or a restaurant server who is very attentive.

GRATITUDE

Turned inward

- Select one small aspect of yourself that you have taken for granted. Bring your mindful awareness to it and feel the emotion of gratitude for this part of yourself.

FINDING BALANCE

Underuse of gratitude

An underuse of gratitude can occur out of a sense of mindlessness or unawareness about life and the good things that occur. Some people have experienced such a degree of hurt that they—consciously or unconsciously—choose not to notice anything remotely uplifting or the goodness of others. In less extreme cases, you might focus so much inwardly that you don't notice people or things in front of you to be grateful for. Another form of underuse occurs when you feel grateful but do not have the emotional or social skills to express that gratitude.

We all miss opportunities here and there to express gratitude for our health, for our relationships, or for our large and small successes, so underuse happens regularly. In particular, we are susceptible to taking those closest to us for granted: our parents, children, siblings, and spouses. An important part of gratitude as a character strength is experiencing and expressing that gratitude to others who deserve to hear it.

Overuse of gratitude

Too much gratitude can seem contrived, repetitive, or annoying to the recipients. It can make some people feel uncomfortable, especially when the recipient is not looking for thanks or does not experience what they've done as special. Others can even come to doubt your sincerity. However, the overly frequent expression of gratitude (profuse gratitude) is more likely to be a very minor annoyance in a relationship rather than a serious problem.

Too much gratitude for what you have in life can also interfere with your reaching for more. Too much focus on gratitude for the positives of a person or situation can interfere with developing perspective on shortcomings, or on pursuing an even better relationship or work situation.

Nicole W., 26, a marketing executive, offers her story on the overuse of gratitude:

I got a divorce at a fairly early age and I became involved pretty quickly with another guy. Gratitude had always been a high strength of mine, so naturally I applied it in my new relationship, which I was especially grateful for because it led me to deflect some of my loneliness and career disappointment at the time. When he would do something nice for me, no matter how small, I would explode with gratitude. Even when he just hung out with me, I experienced gratitude. But over time, I realized gratitude was blinding me to the reality that this guy actually offered me very little. He wasn't very emotionally supportive and didn't have much patience for my struggling to put my life back together. It took me a while to see all of this. Eventually, I realized he wasn't right for me, but it taught me that I need to balance gratitude, being realistic, and caring for myself. I was grateful for him, but I needed to reach a point where that didn't blind me to his serious limitations. After we broke up, I met a much more caring guy, and now I can be both grateful and confident that he's right for me.

GRATITUDE

Optimal use of gratitude:
The golden mean

Gratitude motto:

"I am grateful for many things and I express
that thankfulness to others."

Imagine this:

Imagine that each day of your life you notice at least
three things for which you are grateful, and you express
that gratitude verbally at least once a day to a person, to
nature, to a higher power, or to another living being.

Each time you are aware of feeling gratitude, you take
the time to understand why you are grateful, where it came
from, and how it feels in your body. Each day, you might
feel gratitude for the same things, but you also come up
with three new experiences of gratitude. You realize that
if you were to do this every day for a year you would have
expanded your gratitude in over a thousand ways and would
have verbally practiced sharing it hundreds of times. What
a powerful way to have developed this character strength!

HOPE

WHAT   WHY   HOW

What to Know About Hope

The character strength of hope has to do with positive expectations about the future. It involves optimistic thinking and focusing on good things to come. Hope is more than a feel-good emotion. It is an action-oriented strength involving agency, the motivation and confidence that goals can be reached, and also that many effective pathways can be devised in order to get to that desired future.

Hope and optimism have significant positive consequences for well-being and health. Hope can be directed toward future accomplishments, future relationships (current relationships or new ones), and community-wide or global concerns. Hope is anchored in the present, in the understanding of where things are now, but is sailing toward the future. When others focus on the negative of a situation or respond with indifference or pessimism, a person high in hope is able to provide another perspective and to base those views in a solid, realistic foundation.

Hope is highly correlated with other character strengths linked with well-being. In particular, the relationship between hope and zest is the strongest of any two character strengths. Where zest is an application of positivity to the present, hope is the application of positivity to the future. Hope also tends to be related to gratitude and love. The warmth, appreciation, and energy inherent to these strengths means others find them particularly admirable.

When you are at your best with hope, you maintain a positive outlook on the future and express a balanced, optimistic view that motivates your moving forward and supporting others in the process.

WHAT	WHY	HOW

Why Hope Is Valuable

Research findings on the benefits of hope include the following:

- Hope is one of the two character strengths most associated with life satisfaction and well-being.
- Hope is strongly connected with various elements of well-being, such as heightened pleasure, engagement, meaning, and positive and healthy relationships.
- People who are hopeful are less likely to be anxious or depressed. If they do become anxious or depressed, those feelings tend not to overwhelm them.
- Hopeful people persevere, especially when challenged. They are more resilient.

- Hope and optimism correlate with active problem-solving. Hope is associated with conscientiousness, diligence, and the ability to delay gratification.
- Hopeful people tend to be healthier, happier, and more successful. Hope leads to greater longevity.
- Hope is correlated with lower performance anxiety and better school performance.
- People high in hope retain more positive emotions after a failure.

How to Ignite Your Hope

REFLECTING

Consider these questions as you reflect on your strength of hope:
- What are the conditions that have led you to be hopeful in your life?
- What are the conditions that get in your way of feeling hopeful?
- What role does hope play during challenging times in your life? How do you express hope at those times?
- To what extent does a fear of disappointment or failure temper the degree to which you allow yourself to feel hopeful?
- How do you balance what is realistic and what is unrealistic in terms of your expression of hope and optimism?
- What are the dangers associated with feeling hopeful?

SPOTTING THE STRENGTH

Meet Victoria L., 27, a day care worker:

When I was growing up, there was a civil war in my country. No one in my family died because of it, but I was surrounded by poverty, hunger, and a lot of fear. We would hear gunfire all the time. Around the age of ten or eleven, I started to become aware that most people just seemed to struggle through it all, some people looked defeated by how hard their lives were, and then there were some who had this constant hope within them that something better was coming, and that they could take action to create that better future. Those people seemed to me to be the ones who did the best. Despite everything going on around them, they would glow.

I decided then that that's the kind of person I was going to be. My hope for a better life was what motivated me to take action and come to this country. I took some basic jobs and started putting money together to pay for college. Now I work full-time and do my studies. I could have given up, sat back, and blindly hoped for a rescuer, or just settled for whatever was going to happen. But instead I thought, "I can do this. I can create a better life." I took action, and it's my hope that helped make it all possible for me.

TAKING ACTION

In relationships

- Document three accomplishments with your relationship partner, and consider how each can inspire your relationship in the future.
- Write about your best possible self in a close relationship. Imagine the future in which you are bringing your best possible

242

self forward and you're using your character strengths to make that future a reality.

- The next time one of your close relationships expresses negativity or pessimism, offer them the gift of hopeful comments and ideas. Be concrete and realistic with your expressions of hope. Help the person to identify achievable actions they might take.

At work

- If you can envision how things can work out for the good despite obstacles along the way, and help others to see the same positive possibilities, then you are expressing the strength of hope. Use your strength of hope to work on tasks that will benefit you, your co-workers, or your organization in the long term. Consider how your work today will contribute to the future.
- Set a goal at work for tasks you want to accomplish that day. For any goal you make, consider at least three pathways by which it could be achieved.

Within your community

- Set up a neighborhood or community event around a movie that promotes a message of hope. Examples include *The Shawshank Redemption*, *The Pursuit of Happyness*, and *Pay It Forward*. Include discussions about how the message applies to problems in your community and making a difference.

Turned inward

- Consider a problem or struggle you are having. Write down two optimistic thoughts that bring comfort. Add two actions you can take to move small steps forward.

FINDING BALANCE

Underuse of hope

When you refuse to look to the positive, neglect the good, or reside in the problems of the past or the conflicts in the present, you may be underusing hope. That said, hope can (and perhaps, usually should) be partnered with a recognition of difficulties and obstacles. Hope is not just about belief or a wish; it is about action.

When positive things don't work out—when your hopeful expectations get burned a few too many times—that can lead not just to disappointment but even to resentment about having hope. For some people, reining in their sense of hope can be a way of protecting themselves from disappointment, but this can lapse into sustained pessimism or negativity about the future and its possibilities. A more subtle version of this underuse is the parent who doesn't express much hope for their child's successes because they don't want to set their child up for disappointment or failure. In such cases, the parent is underusing hope rather than combining hope with other character strengths such as perspective or self-regulation.

At other times, hope may be hard to find when you can't see a good reason for optimism about some project. For example, a parent might not know how hard a child has been studying or might not know the good advice friends have been giving them. A boss might not know the extra time an employee is putting in or the work that has been done. The parent or boss is underusing hope, expecting mediocre results or expecting the worst when the reality of the situation is much brighter.

Overuse of hope

While hope is one of the most powerful character strengths for positive feelings, those high in hope need to find some balance. Too much hope can be unrealistic or even "Pollyannaish." *Pollyanna* is an old children's book about a girl who is always positive no matter what. Parents who read the book with their children often say her blind optimism reaches the point that it's annoying. The person who can't imagine or even consider a negative outcome is overplaying hope.

One risk of overuse can be found in the area of physical health. If you receive a serious medical diagnosis and respond only with hope that everything will be all right and don't take action, you could be setting yourself up for serious problems. It's important in this situation to be hopeful about the future, but to not overlook warning signs. This is where using other strengths becomes crucial, such as judgment to evaluate the specifics of the situation, and zest or self-regulation to take effective action.

HOPE

Another example of hope overuse can occur when you set up too many goals or have too many positive expectations. Hopeful people can become overly confident about reaching their goals. This tendency can result in the hopeful person becoming overwhelmed and failing to reach their goals. In these situations, prudence can be an important strength to employ.

When hope is expressed strongly and consistently, it may have an inspirational effect on others. However, expressing more hope than others are ready to hear can annoy others, or lead them to respond with a more pessimistic viewpoint as a counterbalance.

John N., 35, a builder and construction foreman, had this to say about the overuse of hope:

Sometimes when I express a lot of optimism, I notice people roll their eyes. People will sometimes say, "Life can't always be so positive, John." While I realize that, I really can't help trying to find the silver lining in any problem. It makes me wonder if some people question my judgment because of it. It's almost like they think I have my head in the clouds or that I'm just trying to pick flowers and dance in the rain all day long. I strive to achieve some balance with it—to be real. My work can be pretty gritty sometimes, and I just keep going. Sometimes my hope lifts up my team of guys to keep going and tough it out through long hours, and other times it's just annoying to them. It's probably most annoying to them when we're getting a drink after a twelve-hour shift. It's like my hope got everybody through it and now they don't want to hear anything positive anymore; they just want to complain about how hard the day was. That's all right, I get that.

Optimal use of hope:
The golden mean

Hope motto:

"I am realistic and also full of optimism about the future, believing in my actions and feeling confident things will turn out well."

Imagine this:

Imagine yourself one year from today. See yourself as a person happy, confident, and connected to others in your life. Visualize yourself being at your best in your relationships and in your work. Notice the details of how this looks and attend to how it feels to be at your best. This might be very different from how you feel today, or it might be an improvement in the spirit of self-development. Feel a sense of hope right now that you can get to that point in one year. Think about the character strengths that will serve as pathways for you to reach that goal over the coming year. Your hope strength can help lift up these other strengths—to help you see that you can reach this goal of your best self. Notice how your hope can boost your zest for the goal, your perseverance to overcome obstacles, your perspective to keep this bigger picture in mind, and the heart-based strengths of gratitude and love to use along the journey.

HOPE

HUMOR

What to Know About Humor

Humor means to recognize what is amusing in situations, and to offer the lighter side to others. Humor is an important lubricant to social interactions, and can contribute to team building or moving toward group goals. Where other strengths are more or less essential for achieving certain types of goals or dealing with certain types of problems, humor is rarely an essential component to positive social interactions, but it is often a desirable one. It is also a valuable method of coping with distressing situations.

Playfulness is the foundation of humor. Humor is about being able to identify what is absurd or to undermine unnecessary seriousness. Being able to poke fun at yourself is as important to the truly humorous person as being able to make light of the situation. Humor can serve the greater good by bringing levity to difficult situations, by drawing attention to contradictions in life, by sustaining good cheer in the face of despair, and by building social bonds.

It is noteworthy that the loss of a sense of humor seems to cut across virtually all forms of emotional difficulties. This implies that a good sense of humor might not only be a buffer to different kinds of stress and problems, but may also be an important feature of positive mental health. Humor is referred to as a *value-added strength* because it becomes morally good when it is coupled with other strengths. For example, a comedian telling jokes on the stage is unlikely to be morally praiseworthy, but when humor is used to lighten the load for a child with cancer or a lonely elder adult, then humor becomes a morally valued strength.

If you are high in humor, you put people at ease through gentle teasing, playful comments, joking, or funny storytelling, and you don't take yourself too seriously. Other people look to you to break the seriousness of the moment, to lighten a heavy moment, or to give perspective on the relative importance of things. At times, you are considered the life of the party, but can also give voice to what other people are feeling or thinking. You know that constructive feedback, when given with humor, is an easier pill to swallow, and this is one of your important communication tools. You've probably noticed that your humor is contagious in many situations; laughter and lightheartedness, when socially appropriate, can light up the room.

When you are at your best with humor, you see the lighter side of positive, negative, and boring situations, and you are adept at sharing this lightness with others in a way in which the situation calls for it—sometimes playful, sometimes sarcastic, and sometimes with a clever story.

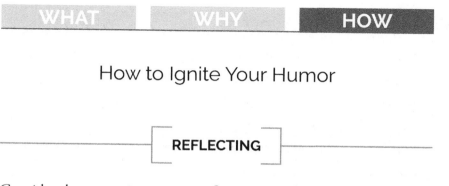

WHAT | **WHY** | **HOW**

Why Humor Is Valuable

Research findings on the benefits of the strength of humor include the following:

- Humorous people are socially attractive to others.
- Humor buffers people from life stress and the hassles of daily living.
- People with a sense of humor tend to be healthier. For example, there are many physiological benefits to laughter, including increased oxygenation of the blood.
- Humor helps enhance pleasure and positive emotions in life, which contribute to overall happiness.
- Humor triggers positive social communication and helps people to appraise situations in a positive way.
- Humor can decrease social anxiety, thereby creating opportunities for social connection.

HUMOR

WHAT | **WHY** | **HOW**

How to Ignite Your Humor

REFLECTING

Consider these questions as you reflect on your strength of humor:

- How do you initiate playfulness, and how does that change from situation to situation?
- How do other people you know express playfulness? What can you learn from observing playfulness in others?
- Timing is critical in being humorous; it is just as important to recognize when not to be funny as it is to recognize when a humorous approach can be valuable. When have you timed your humor poorly, and what led to that?
- What experiences or situations prompt you to give a humorous response?
- How can an awareness of humor be cultivated in your everyday activities?
- Of all your relationships, who do you laugh with the most? How does that humor shape that relationship?
- In what situations has humor been a barrier for you in connecting with others?

SPOTTING THE STRENGTH

Meet Kelvin A., 23, an engineer:

I was shy as a child, and humor has helped me with socializing in general. I've had to do a number of phone-style interviews, and it has helped me seem like a more social person. Humor is part of my way of getting to know people—strangers, distant relatives, and even prospective employers. When I was applying to graduate schools, it was my humor that got me going on the right foot as I started to immediately get to know and connect with the people there. They saw me as being funny and gregarious. As I've gotten older, I've used my humor to meet people in college. It definitely helped me to meet women. If I had stayed rooted in shyness, I would probably never have had a first date with anyone!

Also, I'm proud that I am able to come up with jokes. I think quickly on my feet in situations and am able to say something sarcastic or absurd that fits in the moment. I love it when it catches people off guard and they burst out with a genuine laugh. That's when I've found my zone.

I view humor as a form of intelligence. If someone can make me laugh and I'm impressed by it, I think there's something to that person. Also, I respect people that at least make the effort with a joke. Even if a joke I tell is really bad, my mother will say, "I can't believe you came up with that so quickly." That serves as a reminder to me that I'd rather try to find the funny in the situation than just be serious all the time.

HUMOR

TAKING ACTION

In relationships

- Watch a sitcom or funny movie with a friend or family member who has a strong appreciation of humor.
- Do something spontaneous and playful around another person (e.g., saying something silly, contorting your body in a weird way, or telling a funny story or joke).
- Look for the lighter side of a difficult situation in your relationship. Discuss an appropriate way to bring pleasure and playfulness to the situation.

At work

- If you bring smiles and laughter into the workplace, then you are expressing the strength of humor. Your laughing and smiling can be contagious. Bring a mindful awareness to your laughter and smiling throughout one day at work. At the end of the day, decide whether the frequency was too much, too little, or just right for that particular day.

- Send a funny (socially appropriate, please!) video from YouTube to several of your work colleagues. You might consider the timing of this, and send the video when your co-workers or work team could use a break from a stressful situation.
- Keep a humor diary at work and write down three funny things that happen each day, however small, and why they happened. Share it with others at work after you have a nice collection.

Within your community

- Consider a person in your community who appears lonely or cast aside. Make a point to go up to them and bring them the gifts of smiling and laughter.

Turned inward

- When you find yourself taking life too seriously, pause to turn humor toward yourself and laugh. Allow the levity to fill you up.

FINDING BALANCE

Underuse of humor

There are various reasons why people would be overly serious. Some people underuse humor because they are feeling sick or depressed. Some people just find it uncomfortable to try to be funny; or tend to be serious people; or think they're not good at it; or don't typically view situations with a lens of humor; or assume, rightly or wrongly, that it's socially inappropriate to be funny. For example, you might rightfully assume that humor has no place at a somber funeral, but wrongfully assume that it has no place in relating to your boss. Humor can bring people closer, so underuse can also occur when a normally humorous person distrusts someone or doesn't want to get closer to someone.

Some people are less quick to notice absurdity or other forms of humor in a situation. Others underuse humor because they don't feel confident in their capacity to use this strength.

Overuse of humor

Too much humor can be hurtful and demeaning to others. Many comedians will push the line between what is clever and edgy and what is simply degrading and in poor taste. In relationships, someone high in humor might use humor in an attempt to connect with someone, but misread the cues and instead come across as offensive or uncaring. Humor then leads to the opposite effect: a wedge, conflict, or disconnect in the relationship. This can easily be seen in new relationships, sibling relationships, and even in the young boy who teases a girl because he actually likes her and wants her attention.

Humor can also be a way of avoiding problems and serious issues in life. Some people are especially clever at sensing a challenging topic beginning to emerge and deflecting it with a joke. These people can be particularly annoying to their significant others, as humor can at times be used in a way that the significant other appreciates, but also be a factor that undermines the relationship.

Ava P., 36, a store clerk, had this to say about the overuse of humor:

I like to joke around and see the funny side of pretty much every situation. When I think about it, there are probably times when humor

HUMOR

is not appropriate. I am the person who WILL tell a joke at a funeral. If people don't get that I'm joking, it can be a little awkward.

I wonder if my being funny has prevented people from connecting with me or saying certain things to me. There can be trust issues people might have, or some might see me as less mature than I am because of it. I think they may think I am incapable of taking things seriously and may not see that I can be very thoughtful about solving problems or addressing issues. It's a trade-off.

Some people don't take me as seriously or they think that I don't appreciate things to the full extent. I don't feel there's a lot I can do to fix that. I can squash some of my humor, but I feel that is compromising an important part of who I am. Sometimes I remind people of this and explain that humor and laughter are really important to me. I do think it's important to realize humor has its place.

Optimal use of humor:
The golden mean

Humor motto:

"I approach life playfully, making others laugh, and finding humor in difficult and stressful times."

Imagine this:

Imagine you walk into your work environment and your colleagues are spread around your work area, focusing on tasks, talking with one another, and getting coffee. You walk over to two colleagues having a playful conversation; they're smiling and standing close to each other. You quickly pick up on the stories in the conversation. You make a couple of funny comments and joke about something humorous related to what they've been saying. The group laughs and you head to your desk. An hour later, you write a funny email to your work team that links to a video that you know the team will find hilarious. Later that day, you encounter a co-worker who is visibly upset and stressed about a personal issue. You listen carefully and hold back the urge to use humor early in the conversation. You offer support and friendly comments. When the timing seems right (per your use of your strength of social intelligence), you share a somewhat related but funny story about yourself and a blunder you made. The person receives the joke and laughs, and seems to be uplifted at the moment. When you arrive home, you immediately express yet another type of humor—goofiness and playfulness—because your young children see you and are ready to play.

SPIRITUALITY

WHAT   WHY   HOW

What to Know About Spirituality

As is true for many of the character strengths in the VIA Classification, the strength of spirituality has many dimensions. Some of these include meaning, purpose, life calling, beliefs about the universe, the expression of virtue/goodness, and practices that connect with the transcendent. Spirituality has been defined consistently by scientists as the search for or connection with "the sacred." The sacred might be that which is blessed, holy, revered, or particularly special. This can be secular or non-secular: sacredness might be pursued as the search for a purpose in life or as a close relationship with something greater; the sacred might be experienced in the forgiveness offered by a child, a humble moment between a leader and a subordinate, an awe-inspiring sunset, a profound experience during meditation or a religious service, or the self-sacrificing kindness of a stranger. As a character strength, spirituality involves the belief that there is a dimension to life that is beyond human understanding. Some people don't connect this belief with the concept of a divinity and prefer to think of it in terms of a sense of meaning rather than spirituality, but in the VIA Classification the terms are considered closely related.

Within the VIA Classification, spirituality refers to having coherent beliefs about our place and purpose in the universe and about the meaning of life. These beliefs can shape our relationship with the world around us, shape us as people, and shape our relationships with others. Spirituality is particularly relevant to our style of operating in the world—it is applied to everyday experiences, influencing our conduct and our determination of what is ultimately meaningful. These spiritual beliefs tend to provide personal comfort.

Even among individuals whose spirituality is focused on some sense of divinity, researchers often draw a distinction between spirituality and religiousness. They point out that spirituality refers to the personal, intimate relationship between a human being and the transcendent (e.g., God, a higher power, the sacred, nature, life force, all sentient beings, etc.) as well as the range of virtues that result from that relationship. The practice of spirituality commonly involves contemplation, meditation, prayer, communing with nature, and other practices. It involves having a set of beliefs and emotions representing one's place in the world. Religiousness has more to do with a set of prescribed beliefs and rituals that are associated with the worship of the divine. This usually involves participation in public and private acts of worship, engagement with specific rituals, customs, and readings, and may involve the spiritual practices listed above as well. One need not be religious to be deeply spiritual; it is also common to be religious but not particularly spiritual.

When you are at your best with spirituality, you are accepting and open-minded, regularly express a wide range of virtues in the pursuit of goodness, and use your centeredness to not only connect with the transcendent but also to connect with and appreciate all human beings.

Why Spirituality Is Valuable

Research findings on the benefits of the strength of spirituality include the following:

- Spirituality, through the expression of religiousness or sense of meaning, provides a sense of being grounded, increases optimism, and helps provide a sense of purpose for life. These in turn contribute to an overall sense of well-being.

- People who are spiritual often experience benefits in their physical and psychological health and are resilient in the face of challenges.

- Youth who describe themselves as spiritual show better self-regulation and academic performance, and tend to see the world as a more coherent place.

- Spirituality is associated with the avoidance of risky and rule-breaking behaviors.

- In family life, spirituality is associated with lower levels of marital conflict, greater perceived spousal support, more consistent parenting, and more supportive relationships between children and their parents.

- Spirituality has also been linked with many character strengths, including humility, forgiveness, gratitude, kindness, hope, love, and zest. Looking at specific types of behaviors, it is also connected to compassion, altruism, volunteerism, and philanthropy.

SPIRITUALITY

WHAT	WHY	HOW

How to Ignite Your Spirituality

REFLECTING

Consider these questions as you reflect on your strength of spirituality:

- What positive role (relationships, health, achievement, community involvement) does spirituality or a sense of meaning play in your life?
- How do you define spirituality for yourself?
- How is spirituality related to your religious practices or lack thereof?
- How does spirituality affect your relationships with others?
- What role has spirituality played during challenging times in your life?
- To what extent do you feel that there is one true way to be spiritual for all people as opposed to people finding their own way?
- Do the beliefs and behaviors that are the expressions of your spirituality cause problems in your life; for example, in relationships, at work, or elsewhere?

SPOTTING THE STRENGTH

Meet Jacob L., 24, a social worker:

There's something to being on a schedule that I like. I like order in my life, and religion has always given me that. In terms of my religion, I'm an Orthodox Jew. I've always felt a sense of comfort in the idea of being close to God. There's an interesting dynamic between my being religious and my sense of spirituality. For me, they're not the same thing. The religion is about being part of a community, but there's an aspect of spirituality that is individualized. How do you live in a world where you're seeking a personal, private relationship with a Creator, but you also want to be connected socially to other people who have that relationship as well? How do you do that dance? Maybe that challenge is why so many people today think of themselves as "spiritual but not religious."

I do find a great deal of spirituality in the religion itself. There can be great moments in connecting as part of a community. In fact, I think I'm naturally drawn to being a hermit, and my interest in religion is a way of connecting to community. Judaism is a particularly communal religion. My natural inclination is very introverted and personally spiritual, and religion has helped me become more extroverted. It's enriched me in a lot of ways in that sense. It has forced me to get out of my shell.

The other part of this has been my connection to religious texts. I find that reading and contemplating religious texts is a highly spiritual relationship. There's a depth to religious texts that I find brings me spiritual fulfillment. I didn't like going to religious school, but there were certain times I unlocked something in a story and saw it in a deeper, more spiritual and meaningful way that meant a lot to me. It actually gave me purpose.

SPIRITUALITY

TAKING ACTION

In relationships

- How is your closest relationship sacred? Discuss this question with that person.

- Engage in a spiritual experience with one of your close relationships—this might be meditation, contemplation, prayer, or doing a particular ritual together.
- Create your own spiritual ceremony for an important event or transition in life. You might create a sacred ceremony for the birth of a child, for the transition to or from high school, or as a relationship ritual renewing your vows on your wedding day each year.

At work

- Place a symbol or meaningful object at your desk that reminds you of the sacredness of life or reflects your spirituality or religion. Periodically look over at the object, close your eyes, and either practice mindful breathing, offer a prayer, repeat a mantra or meditate, or just reflect on what matters most to you.
- Find meaning at work—consider what matters most in the work you do and the impact it has upon others. Pause to appreciate this.

Within your community

- Think of a spiritual role model in your community. Even if there are important differences between their beliefs and yours, consider their best qualities and one way you might learn from them.
- Look for a sacred space in your community environment. This can be a place of religious worship, or a beautiful place in a park, perhaps even a mall where the bustle reveals something meaningful to you about community. Spend time in that space, find ways to improve it, and involve others.

Turned inward

- Pause to connect with the sacred within, what some refer to as your inner spirit. Return to this solitude that resides within throughout the day. Breathe deeply and be at peace with yourself.

FINDING BALANCE

Underuse of spirituality

Like all the character strengths, spirituality is multidimensional. It refers to having meaning, purpose, beliefs about the interconnectedness of life, living by virtues of goodness, having a faith in something greater, and/or religious beliefs and practices. A person who doesn't bring any of these to bear in life can be viewed as underusing spirituality. Some people might feel lost and without meaning, others might feel betrayed or disappointed by a particular religion, and others are simply uninterested in connecting with abstract ideas like transcendence in any way. Remember that we are not equating atheism (or agnosticism) with underuse of spirituality. It's common for atheists to connect with the sacred in their lives, to find events have a greater meaning for them, and/or to engage in rituals that have a spiritual component. It is possible to find deep meaning in the clockwork nature of the universe, the mystery of fate, universal truths about human nature, or even the beauty of mathematics.

People who are devoutly religious—attending services and engaging in rituals daily—might be underusing their spirituality if they are engaging in their religion mindlessly or if they don't deliberately apply virtues in their daily life. The common example is the couple

SPIRITUALITY

who attend a church service every Sunday and in the parking lot cut off other drivers, curse out people walking slowly, and yell at one another. Clearly, they are underusing spirituality in this situation (among other strengths).

The underuse of spirituality can also be seen in mindless daily life and routine. In many situations, it can seem as if the person is oblivious to any kind of life meaning or depth around them. When it is pointed out that the preciousness of life can be found in any present moment or routine, this is often a wake-up call for that person.

Overuse of spirituality

The expression of too much spirituality or religiousness can be mildly annoying or intensely disturbing. Those who overuse this strength usually believe they are using the strength in a magnanimous and helpful way. Others will often perceive the overuse of spirituality as preachy, misguided, ungrounded, self-righteous, or narrow-minded. At the extreme, spirituality can lapse into fanaticism, a tendency to force spirituality on others. This can be a common hot button for people on the receiving end of overuse, leaving them feeling irritated by the person. This can lead to a break in the relationship and avoidance of the person overusing the strength.

The overuse of spirituality can reflect a lack of critical thinking and judgment about the variety of expressions of religion and spirituality. Spirituality at its best tends to be associated with the recognition that no one person or religion has the final truth. This recognition can be an expression of the strength of humility, a strength that is valued by many religions.

It is also possible to pursue a sense of meaning excessively. Some individuals may look for meaning to such a degree that they lose sight of their relationships or their responsibilities to others. In some cases, the person may expect mystical, transcendent, or very meaningful experiences throughout the day. When those experiences don't occur, they can become disappointed or cynical about the search for personal meaning.

Isabel A., 34, a bookseller, offered her story about the overuse of spirituality:

I grew up in a religious home. My father was a clergyman. My family went to religious services a couple of times every week and participated in rituals each day in our home life. We used sacred texts and readings which had the final say in everything—in our problems, conflicts, even our joys and sorrows. I was repeatedly told that I should share my religion with others and convince them to consider a similar path. I was pretty young when I took this on in my community. I remember most of the kids just sort of looking at me funny or ignoring me. A couple asked a question or two. As I grew up, I began to meet people outside of my community. Most didn't think the way I did. I was always told this approach in life would fulfill me and answer all my questions. But when I was really honest with myself, I realized it didn't. It was not enough. And, I had been told I can't say that—I can't say "it's not enough." But it wasn't.

I began to listen to how others expressed their religious or spiritual views. I engaged in practices from other traditions. I challenged my beliefs. I haven't rejected all the beliefs from my childhood, but I've matured and grown in my spiritual perspective. I feel I've become a lot more open-minded and accepting of others' views. I'm actually more caring for all people now.

SPIRITUALITY

Spirituality motto:

"I feel spiritual and believe in a sense of purpose or meaning in my life; and I see my place in the grand scheme of the universe and find meaning in everyday life."

Imagine this:

Whether you are religious, spiritual, both, or neither, imagine intending to build more of the spirituality strength in your life. You realize that there are many paths to pursuing or tapping into the transcendent. You view the search for and the experience of meaning in your everyday life and your relationships as particularly important. You have beliefs that support this journey and how you and others fit in the grand scheme of life and death.

See yourself as being attentive to the sacredness of each moment of your life. You engage in practices such as meditation, yoga, prayer, readings of spiritual texts, or simple contemplation as a way to connect more deeply with what's sacred inside you, to connect more deeply with others in relationships, and to connect more deeply with "something greater" that connects you with all of life. See yourself using all 24 of your character strengths, including but not limited to gratitude, hope, zest, love, and kindness, and how using all your strengths can help you to contribute to greater goodness in the world.

PUTTING IT ALL TOGETHER

This section has offered you a wide range of ways you can understand your character strengths. Growing your character strengths is not like learning to ride a bike—once you learn it, you've got it. Rather, it is an ongoing journey. You learn, challenge yourself, experiment, discuss, and play with your strengths. You bring them strongly and mindfully to each situation in your life—from handling a tense argument with your loved one to sticking with a work project or helping to clean up a park in your community. Through the mundane (e.g., brushing your teeth) to the inspiring (e.g., viewing a panoramic mountain scene), your character strengths will be there. Through the positive experiences (e.g., having coffee with an old friend) to the troubled times (e.g., experiencing the loss of a family member), your character strengths will be there.

They've been there, available for you to use them, in every moment of your life. They're there as you read these words. And, they're there as you consider your next step in taking action in your life.

There is a multitude of resources on character strengths to support you on your journey. Each offers a complement to this book. The best place to start is to take time to review all the tabs on the VIA Institute website (www.viacharacter.org)—the global headquarters for all-things-character. In addition to taking the VIA Survey to assess (or reassess) your strengths, you can find videos, articles, and strategies on character strengths. There are live and on-demand courses and personalized reports to help you make character strengths personal and to deepen your understanding of character strengths and expand your strengths practice.

If you're a professional helping others make the most of their character strengths, then you'll want to get one of the go-to, popular books for practitioners on the topic—*Character Strengths Interventions: A Field-Guide for Practitioners* (Hogrefe, 2018), or *Mindfulness and Character Strengths: A Practical Guide to Flourishing* (Hogrefe, 2014).

For now, turn your attention to Part III, where you'll find *Strengths Builder,* an easy-to-follow, research-backed program in four steps to work on your character strengths. This will help you go from present reality to thriving, taking your knowledge and practice to the next level!

PART III:

Strengths Builder

Thriving with Your Character Strengths:
A Four-Step Program

Part I of this book offered you an introduction to the VIA Classification of character strengths. Part II reviewed each of the character strengths in detail. Now we move to Part III, in which we introduce the research-based **Strengths Builder**. *Strengths Builder* will help you create a *strengths practice* that takes your strengths to the next level!

Strengths Builder draws on the latest science concerning how to grow and nourish your character strengths. It will help you put the character strengths, concepts, practices, and research from Parts I and II into a daily, sustainable practice. What you've read to this point is more descriptive and informal; you can pick and choose what you use. *Strengths Builder* is a more structured approach to appreciating and developing your character strengths. The goal is to apply the strengths to create a more thriving life. To thrive is to function at our best, making the most of opportunities and learning from and managing adversities. It means you are creating opportunities and positive experiences while handling difficulties with resilience. This four-step program will help you make the most of your best inner-most qualities: your strengths of character.

These exercises have been shared in various forms with thousands of people around the world who have attended workshops or lectures, participated in remote courses, or engaged in individual work with us, and feedback has been very positive. We've seen firsthand the benefits that come from these and similar exercises involving character strengths.

Fostering self-care: *Strengths Builder* is a new form of self-care. It offers you a pathway to give support and sustenance to yourself. We would argue that working on your strengths in such a way has the potential to be as important to your well-being as other contributors to health, such as a healthy diet, quality sleep, and regular exercise. These strengths help us foster a healthy personal well-being that can positively affect us physically, mentally, emotionally, socially, and spiritually. This is a well-being that can quickly spread socially and make a positive impact on others.

Your strengths practice: Each step is built around a particular activity. The use of strengths to move toward thriving is a matter of practice. It is *your* practice. We're not saying you will ever reach perfection in your use of the strengths; we're saying that the more you practice using your strengths effectively and thoughtfully (mindfully), the more naturally strengths use will come to you. In that way, practicing with character strengths is no different from practicing the guitar or piano, practicing to play basketball or soccer, practicing yoga or meditation, or keeping up with an exercise routine. Stick with the exercises that make up the four steps, continue to practice them, and you are not only solidly on your way to thriving, but you're also creating an approach to life that is sustainable over time. In following the four steps that make up *Strengths Builder*—one step per week—you will be creating your strengths practice by discovering, exploring, and using your character strengths in exciting new ways. The four steps are:

1. Recognizing and appreciating strengths in others.
2. Exploring and using your signature strengths.
3. Applying your strengths to life challenges.
4. Making strengths a habit.

Track your progress: At each step, space is provided for you to explore your insights and experiences on the topic. After the description, examples, and initial exploration, you will find a one-page tracking sheet at the end of each step. This is the central place to record your daily activities involving your strengths use. For those of you reading this electronically, use the notes feature of your reader or an external note-taking device to write this information down. Each section will outline what you want to include in those notes. We strongly recommend you write down your thoughts from each step rather than just thinking about them. You may find it helpful to be able to return later to what you wrote. Sometimes rereading what you wrote will spark all sorts of new thoughts about your strengths.

Go at your own pace: Though we envision each step taking a week, for a total of four weeks, the program is self-guided. Decide for yourself whether you want to spend extra time on a particular step depending on your schedule, your other commitments, and the insights you experience. The greatest benefit comes when the steps are completed in sequence. However, as you move forward, you may find you want to return to previous exercises with fresh eyes or to deepen your practice. Remember, working on your character strengths is a journey, not a destination. Take your time as you learn and grow, and be sure to have fun!

Consider partnering with a buddy: There's no doubt that personal growth and behavior change benefit from the support of others. Go through *Strengths Builder* with a friend, family member, or work colleague. This is likely to increase your accountability, planning, and follow-through with the activities. Of course, if you prefer, taking action alone works well for many people too.

Consider a helping professional: Many people who use *Strengths Builder* for themselves will find that they want to help others, such as their family members, significant others, clients, patients, students, and employees. This may indeed be a good approach to help others activate their strengths, boost their well-being, and overcome stressors and life challenges. It is not meant to replace the help of a mental health, medical, or coaching professional for those struggling with a significant mental health or other serious problem. In those cases, a professional should be considered. *Strengths Builder* can serve as a strong additional support to be discussed with the professional.

First, take the VIA Survey: If you haven't done so already, before starting this program, take the VIA Survey at

www.viacharacter.org

Have your free, multi-page VIA Survey results handy as you proceed through each step.

While you work through *Strengths Builder*, be sure to turn to Part II of this book for additional insights and activities that support each of the 24 strengths.

Let's begin.

Recognizing and Appreciating Strengths in Others

Week 1/Step 1

An important first step in using character strengths more effectively is to observe them in others. We call this exercise "strengths-spotting." This means you actively and regularly look for the strengths in the actions and words of people around you. Most people find it easier to spot strengths in others than in themselves. It is a simple and energizing experience for both the spotter and the receiver when you share what you have observed with them. It sets forth your strengths practice journey in a positive and reinforcing way. This is why week 1/step 1 begins by looking for strengths outside of yourself.

Strengths-spotting is helpful in several ways. First, it will make you more aware of other people's strengths, and of how often people are using those strengths every day. Second, it will help you build your "strengths vocabulary," your ability to identify and describe strengths. Third, it will help you become more appreciative of the strengths of others. You're likely to find yourself complimenting others more on their strengths, pointing out to others when you see them demonstrating their strengths, and helping them become more aware of the strengths that are most important to them. These behaviors are likely to improve your relationships with people who are important to you. In later exercises, you'll apply these same tools of recognition, appreciation, and increased understanding to yourself. As you become more fluent with this language of strengths, you will become better at seeing the best qualities in yourself and in others.

This is an important first step in enriching your strengths use. By labeling the strengths, thinking of them as objective elements of who you are as a person, you become more aware of your strengths. In subsequent steps, you can then use those strengths in the process of creating a more flourishing life.

There are two parts to this week's strengths-spotting exercise: recognizing strengths in TV or other media characters, and recognizing and expressing appreciation for the strengths of people in your life.

Days 1–2: Strengths-Spotting in the Media

Every day it seems we spend time gazing at various media: movies, television, books, YouTube videos, Facebook status updates, tweets. Looking for strengths in someone you don't know personally will help you ease into a good habit. And, you'll quickly see that character strengths can be found all around you and in anyone, anywhere!

For the first two days this week, consider your current interests. What TV series are you currently watching? What fiction or nonfiction book are you reading right now? Maybe there is a television news anchor, a game show host, a popular blogger you read, a character (cartoon or fictional), or a celebrity that you or others in your family admire? Choose one character or person and list at least two of their top strengths from the list of twenty-four (remember, they're at the beginning of this book and in your character strengths profile). Then, write out the rationale for each strength you have spotted. In other words, what's the evidence you have for that strength in that person or character?

Days 3–7: Strengths-Spotting and Strengths Appreciating in Others

Your strengths-spotting practice in the media world will set the stage for something more important: strengths-spotting in your relationships. Positive relationships are viewed by many scientists as the most important contributor to greater happiness, and there is even evidence that it is the single most important contributor to life expectancy as you age. Your recognition of character strengths in others can contribute tremendously to creating, sustaining, and nurturing meaningful relationships! For the remainder of the week, observe the positive in others. Practice spotting the character strengths of anyone you interact with: members of your family, your intimate partner, children, neighbors, a supervisor, colleagues at work, teammates, other students, fellow volunteers or group members (yes, even social media contacts). You might notice an older neighbor sweeping their front porch, a pattern they follow every morning with gusto, and you see perseverance or zest evident in their behavior. You might hear your partner review how they organized their workday, and in their words you may hear the strengths of leadership, teamwork, prudence, perseverance, self-regulation, or judgment. Maybe your child runs up to you giggling and points out your untucked, coffee-stained shirt, and it will make you think about how they use their humor to bond with others.

Observe at least one person per day. Listen to their story, notice their actions, and attend to the positives in how they're dealing with their day. As you did with media, note at least two of the character strengths you see them use and the evidence that supports your observation. Then, take this one step further by conveying your appreciation to the person for their strength use. To express appreciation, consider why you admire that strength in them, why it's of value to you, or how it positively influences you or others. Consider if the strength use inspires you, attracts you, or helps you connect with the person. Perhaps you appreciate the strength because it contributes to a stronger team, neighborhood, company, classroom, or family?

Here's one example of appreciation being expressed: "I see the strength of hope in you—you quickly turned that stressful situation into a positive story about where it will lead for the team. I really value that strength in you. It inspires all of us to be more resilient when times are tough. Thank you." Nonverbal expressions of appreciation may include a pat on the back or a handshake.

WEEK 1 STEP 1	Character Strengths: Who are you observing? What top strengths are you observing in that person? (minimum = two strengths)	Description: Give reasons/ explanations for the strengths you are spotting.	Appreciation: How will you express to the person that you value their strengths?
Day 1 – movie, show, book			
Day 2 – movie, show, book			
Day 3 – person			
Day 4 – person			
Day 5 – person			
Day 6 – person			
Day 7 – person			

Exploring and Using Your Signature Strengths

Week 2/Step 2

Examine the free results you received after completing the VIA Survey. This personalized list shows the 24 strengths listed from highest to lowest. There are many ways you can examine your results. Let's break the strengths into three general categories:

1. Signature strengths: These are your highest strengths and are characterized by "the three e's": they are likely the most *energizing*, they are *easy* for you to use, and they are *essential* to who you are. Just like your personal signature, these *signature strengths* are at the core of your identity. They are uniquely you. While the number of signature strengths can vary between people, a general rule of thumb is to target your top five, but the actual number can vary from four to seven.

2. Lower, or lesser, character strengths: These are your bottom five strengths. These are not weaknesses; they are strengths you probably haven't practiced as much or given as much deliberate attention to.

3. Middle, or supportive, character strengths: These are the remaining fourteen or so strengths residing in the middle of your profile. These offer support for your other strengths.

It is normal (and very tempting) to spend time feeling bothered about your lesser strengths. It is important to remember that the VIA Survey is measuring strengths. Lower scores on these strengths just means less reliance on that strength, not a personal weakness. A way to consider these lesser strengths is as elements of effective functioning that have received less attention from you, or that may not be as important to how you function in the world as the other strengths. It's OK to examine these lesser strengths in yourself and consider whether to enhance them. However, research shows that the time we spend understanding, appreciating, and expressing our highest strengths of character yields the highest benefit. In fact, recent studies have shown that using your signature strengths more leads to greater well-being and flourishing and less depression. Signature strengths will be our focus in step two.

Ready to dig into your signature strengths? Take a few minutes to understand and reflect on each signature strength. Reread the section in Part II on each of your signature strengths. Consider the connection of the strength to you, how each signature strength displays itself in your daily life. Remember the three e's: ask yourself how *energizing* it is to use that strength, how *easy* it is to use, and how *essential* it is to who you are.

There are three questions to explore for each strength. The first question helps you understand the "signature-ness" of each of your top strengths. It allows you to confirm, endorse, appreciate, and if you're ready, positively *accept* this aspect of who you are. The second question helps you to link your signature strength with your values, your relationships, your life purpose, and/or your personal goals. The third question brings you to see that the result of using this strength is not always positive: sometimes there can be "too much of a good thing." By reflecting on the potential costs of using the strength, you begin to understand situations in which you might overuse it.

Space is provided for you to answer these questions for your top five strengths. You might find it helpful to address the same questions for other strengths near the top of your profile. This exploration is beneficial for developing deeper self-awareness of, insights into, and appreciation for your best qualities.

Character strength #1: _____

How does this character strength describe the real me? In what ways is it a true description of me?

_____

_____

_____

_____

How is this strength of value to me? Why is it important for me?

_____

_____

_____

_____

What are the costs of this strength for me? In what ways does it not serve me well?

_____

_____

_____

_____

Character strength #2: _____

How does this character strength describe the real me? In what ways is it a true description of me?

_____

_____

_____

_____

How is this strength of value to me? Why is it important for me?

_____

_____

_____

_____

What are the costs of this strength for me? In what ways does it not serve me well?

_____

_____

_____

_____

Character strength #3: _____

How does this character strength describe the real me? In what ways is it a true description of me?

_____

_____

_____

_____

How is this strength of value to me? Why is it important for me?

_____

_____

_____

_____

What are the costs of this strength for me? In what ways does it not serve me well?

_____

_____

_____

_____

Character strength #4: _____

How does this character strength describe the real me? In what ways is it a true description of me?

_____

_____

_____

_____

How is this strength of value to me? Why is it important for me?

_____

_____

_____

What are the costs of this strength for me? In what ways does it not serve me well?

_____

_____

_____

_____

Character strength #5: _____

How does this character strength describe the real me? In what ways is it a true description of me?

_____

_____

_____

_____

How is this strength of value to me? Why is it important for me?

_____

_____

_____

_____

What are the costs of this strength for me? In what ways does it not serve me well?

_____

_____

_____

_____

Now it's time to take this to the next level. Studies have repeatedly shown that it's the *use* of your character strengths that really matters for boosting your well-being. Using your character strengths is where you gain the biggest benefit and a greater likelihood of flourishing and boosting your engagement in what's going on around you. In other words, *move from your head to positive action!*

How might you take action? A number of research studies have shown that a beneficial way to take action is to use your signature strengths in a new way each day—to *expand* the use of your signature strengths. You might be accustomed to doing kind acts for your family, but to do something kind for a co-worker might be new to you. Maybe your curiosity already emerges when it comes to trying new foods or traveling to new places, but you don't use it much in asking questions of people in your life. The number of new ways we can use our signature strengths in new ways is virtually limitless.

Days 1–2: Reflecting on Past Uses of Signature Strengths

After you've answered the preceding questions about your signature strengths, getting to know your signature strengths better, spend the next two days reflecting on how you have used your signature strengths in the past. Consider a situation in the last couple of weeks in which you used one or more of your signature strengths in a way that made the situation better. Perhaps you used humor to act silly during your morning routine and it lightened your day, or perhaps you brought social intelligence to a team meeting and that led you to make a nice contribution. Be sure to consider how your strengths use benefited you and/or others. Maybe you felt a closer connection to someone, felt a positive boost to your mood, or noticed that people around you became more focused in what they were doing.

Days 3–7: New Uses of Signature Strengths

Each day for the rest of the week, challenge yourself to use one of your signature strengths in a new way, however small. Think about how you use one of your signature strengths regularly in your life: how might you expand upon this, direct it to a new situation, use it with a "new" person? Could you use it to help boost one of your other strengths? For example, if you have problems with perseverance, try using social intelligence to convince someone to help you persevere on a project, or use hope to energize yourself to persist.

Another potential pathway is to use a different aspect of the strength (examine the character strength definitions to get new ideas). For example, if it's the "nice and friendly" part of kindness that you tend to display, think about how to show kindness to someone through generosity, or through the expression of deep compassion, or just through paying someone a compliment. If humor is one of your signature strengths, you could expand your use by finding something humorous in a new setting or with a new person (such as the cashier at the grocery store), or you can think of how to use a different aspect of humor. For example, you may never have used humor to lighten a tense situation before, or to make someone shy feel more comfortable.

Most people stick with the same signature strength throughout the week for this exercise, but it's OK if you decide to change the signature strength you're focusing on to offer yourself new insights.

WEEK 2 STEP 2	Signature Strengths: What strength are you focusing on?	Description: How did you use the signature strength in the situation?	Benefits: What benefits for you or others resulted from the strengths use?
Day 1 – reflecting on past use			
Day 2 – reflecting on past use			
Day 3 – use in a new way today			
Day 4 – use in a new way today			
Day 5 – use in a new way today			
Day 6 – use in a new way today			
Day 7 – use in a new way today			

Applying Your Strengths to Life Challenges

Week 3/Step 3

Despite our best intentions to focus on strengths, our minds can quickly be overcome by challenges, difficulties, problems, and conflicts. Sometimes these are minor. Other times we can become stuck in our problems and our bad habits. It rarely occurs to us to turn to our best qualities to help, but we can often use our signature strengths to bring us back into balance and provide a new perspective on our challenges.

This week the focus will zoom in on using strengths, especially your signature strengths, to manage life challenges.

Before targeting a current life challenge, take a moment to look at a past success with a problem or situation. Your character strengths were there, whether you knew it at the time or not. See for yourself.

Name a problem, stressor, or conflict that you successfully overcame or resolved. This might be an issue from a month ago or a year ago, and it can be a big or small problem, but the main point is that it's something you fully resolved and overcame. Please describe it here:

_____

_____

_____

_____

_____

Looking back to that time, what character strengths did you use to manage or resolve it? What was it inside you that helped you deal with the problem, manage it, stick with it? You might want to review each of the 24 character strengths and their definitions in your character strengths profile closely before giving your response. Write out the main character strengths you activated and the way in which you used each one. We've provided space for three, but feel free to add more. In fact, we encourage you to stretch to think of as many strengths as you can that you used in that situation.

Character strength #1: _____

How did you use this strength to address this challenge?

_____

_____

_____

Character strength #2:

How did you use this strength to address this challenge?

_____

_____

_____

Character strength #3:

How did you use this strength to address this challenge?

_____

_____

_____

Once again, this week will be devoted to two activities. Most of the week will be spent on using character strengths with hassles, irritants, and conflicts in your day. At the end of the week, the focus will turn to the use of your strengths to bring benefit to others.

Days 1–5: Using Strengths with a Challenge

Everyone experiences various daily hassles and tensions. Think of everyday challenges and hassles that confront you: overeating at dinner, doing the dishes, talking to an annoying co-worker, learning to play an instrument, driving in traffic, arguing with a spouse, feeling bored. If you have trouble coming up with ideas, consider what tends to get you frustrated, upset, irritated, disappointed, nervous, guilty, or sad. Each of those feelings is probably connected with certain situations you could use in this exercise. The next step will be to consider how you can handle the challenge that day using one or more of your signature strengths. As you take action with your strengths, you can remind yourself that your strengths are there to energize the experience, and may even make it more manageable and fun.

Days 6–7: Using Strengths to Benefit Others

Strengths are not only beneficial for you but also can help others. For the end of your week, keep up the same approach of using strengths with a challenge each day, but for these last two days consider how you could use your signature strengths to benefit other people who are facing a challenge. How could you use your strengths to help others? Think about someone or a group that you know is facing a challenge. Think about how using *your* signature strengths could help them address that challenge more effectively.

This exercise may involve moving out of your comfort zone, feeling an increase in stress, pressure, or the unknown as you help others. Along with such tensions, you may notice positive emotions and sensations that are commonly felt when doing something good for others.

WEEK 3 STEP 3	Situation: What is the situation in which you are using your character strengths?	Character Strengths: Which strengths did you use?	Explanation: How did you use your strengths to overcome/ manage the challenge OR how did you use strengths to help others?	Benefits/ Results: What happened for you or the people around you as a result of the strengths use?
Day 1 – use with a challenge				For you:
Day 2 – use with a challenge				For you:
Day 3 – use with a challenge				For you:
Day 4 – use with a challenge				For you:
Day 5 – use with a challenge				For you:
Day 6 – use with a challenge in a way that benefits others				For others:
Day 7 – use with a challenge in a way that benefits others				For others:

Making Strengths a Habit

Week 4/Step 4

Begin week four by taking stock of your progress so far. Take a look at both your character strengths profile and at your insights across the last three weeks. Appreciate the insights and changes you have achieved so far. In the first three weeks, you have increased your ability to spot and appreciate strengths in others, to see them more clearly in yourself, and to use them in both good and difficult situations. There's a good chance you are ready to make a habit out of your strengths use!

What stands out most to you so far across the three weeks? What is it that you would most like to build on or change? Make a list of goals you would like that involve making improvements on your strengths awareness and use. As you brainstorm, don't hold back and don't judge what pops up! Consider all 24 of your character strengths. Here are some possibilities:

- You may see a goal that involves using a strength more often. For example, you may decide you want to use self-regulation more to help you make wiser food choices when you are looking for a snack.

- You may see a goal that involves using a certain strength in a different way. For example, you may realize you've never used humor to deal with an issue in your relationship with your partner, or used forgiveness to feel less frustrated at the supermarket.

- You may see a goal that involves using a strength in combination with another strength. For example, in your leadership work you may think it would be helpful to use prudence to react less strongly when you disagree.

- You may even see a goal that would lead you to use a certain strength less. For example, you may decide you use humor too much in conflict situations, or that your tendency to forgive too quickly has undermined your standing up for yourself.

Be sure to consider all areas of your life—health, relationships, spirituality/meaning, and so on. Imagine that each goal you brainstorm would have a sentence that starts like this: "I would like to . . ."

Once you have identified your goal or goals, you can pave your way to your goal using a technique that researchers refer to as *implementation intentions*. Implementation intentions have to do with anticipating both opportunities and obstacles that can arise while you're pursuing your goal. Are there things that may happen that will make it easier to achieve your goal, or things that will make it harder? Implementation intentions are "if-then" plans that spell out in advance how you will respond when good or bad things come up as you move toward your goal. For example, suppose you are working toward a goal of using creativity more. One possibility you anticipate is that a co-worker will reject your use of creativity. Here is the implementation intention you may form in this situation:

- *If* I feel upset by someone rejecting my use of creativity (obstacle), *then* I will remind myself that it's good that I use honesty to express myself authentically.

Suppose you know that a new project may be starting soon at work, and that this project will give you an opportunity to be creative in a new way. The implementation intention here might be something like this:

- *If* I hear the project is being set up (opportunity), *then* I will be brave and ask my co-worker if I can help contribute to it, and I will use social intelligence to think about how best to present my case to them.

What we encourage you to do is to think about the possible obstacles you will face in approaching any of your goals, and then think about which strengths can be marshaled to help you overcome that obstacle. Similarly, think of possible opportunities that will move you toward your goal, then think about which strengths can be marshaled to help you make the most of that opportunity. These implementation intentions can both help you overcome obstacles that might otherwise have shut down your goal and take advantage of opportunities you might otherwise have missed.

Days 1–7: Strength-Based Activities to Achieve My Goals

For this final week, select one of the strengths-oriented goals you brainstormed earlier as a focal point for the week. Each day, you will engage in one activity that contributes to that goal and moves you another step forward in accomplishing it. For example, suppose your goal is to spend more quality time with your family. A goal-oriented activity one day might be to use your curiosity to find out what everyone's favorite group activities are; another day the activity may be to use love to listen to and connect with each family member; and another day you might use leadership to arrange an outing for everyone.

For each daily activity, you'll think of obstacles that might impede your progress, and the opportunities that might emerge (the *ifs*), and how you'll respond to both obstacles and opportunities using your character strengths (the *thens*). Note that you might wish to do the same activity more than once during the week. Keep this list of implementation intentions with you during the day as you pursue your goal. Reread it as you work on the activity for that day so you're ready when the obstacles and opportunities arise. Don't worry too much if you face an unexpected obstacle or opportunity—that's inevitable! But now that you're thinking in terms of implementation intentions and strengths, you'll be better equipped to handle those surprises and unique situations.

By the end of this week, you'll be well on your way to establishing a routine with your strengths use. You might be ready to choose another goal, continue with the same one, or make some tweaks to your process. Stick with it! You are on a path to sustainable strengths growth and meaningful progress on your life goals.

MY CHARACTER STRENGTHS GOAL

This week, I want to _____

_____

	Activities: What action will you take toward your goal today? When? Where?	Obstacles ("if…"): What obstacles might get in the way? (list 1–2 "ifs")	Opportunities ("if…"): What positive opportunities might arise? (list 1–2 "ifs")	Your response ("then…"): Which character strengths will you use to respond to each "if" you identified?
WEEK 4 **STEP 4**				
Day 1				
Day 2				
Day 3				
Day 4				
Day 5				
Day 6				
Day 7				

SOME FINAL THOUGHTS

We hope we have introduced you to a new way of thinking about yourself, your life, and the lives of others. So much of the time, we focus on our faults and our flaws, as well as the failings of others. A character strengths-based approach provides an exciting new perspective for thinking about the challenges and joys of life. We can instead confront our struggles as a matter of better using our strengths rather than solely focusing on overcoming our weaknesses. You are a person of strength. You have a wealth of character strength potential you can ignite. You can appreciate and celebrate that in yourself. You can positively impact the important people in your life. You can use those strengths to reach the goals you have set for yourself. *Strengths Builder* is meant to start you on this life-enhancing journey. We hope this journey helps you to thrive, to discover newfound resilience to face the struggles in your life, and to uncover the many joys in the positive.

REFERENCES/RECOMMENDATIONS BOOKS ON CHARACTER STRENGTHS

Core books

Character Strengths and Virtues: A Handbook and Classification, by Christopher Peterson and Martin Seligman (New York, NY/Washington, DC: Oxford University Press/American Psychological Association, 2004).

This 800-page scholarly tome is the original scientific publication on the VIA Classification of Character Strengths and Virtues.

Character Strengths Interventions: A Field-Guide for Practitioners, by Ryan Niemiec (Boston: Hogrefe, 2018).

This is positive psychology's first field guide, citing hundreds of character strengths studies while offering easy-to-understand, practical models and tools for any helping professional, including nearly 100 handouts for practitioner and client use.

Specific topics

Stress: *The Strengths-Based Workbook for Stress Relief,* by Ryan Niemiec (Oakland: New Harbinger, 2019).

Mindfulness: *Mindfulness and Character Strengths,* by Ryan Niemiec (Boston: Hogrefe, 2014).

Work: *Your Strengths Blueprint,* by Michelle McQuaid and Erin Lawn (Albert Park, Victoria: Michelle McQuaid, 2014).

Movies: *Positive Psychology at the Movies 2,* by Ryan Niemiec and Danny Wedding (Boston: Hogrefe, 2014).

General: *Character Strengths Matter,* by Shannon Polly and Kathryn Britton (Charleston: Positive Psychology News LLC, 2015).

Coaching: *Authentic Strengths,* by Fatima Doman (Las Vegas: Next Century Publishing, 2016).

Parenting: *The Strengths Switch,* by Lea Waters (Australia: Penguin Random House Australia, 2017).

Couples relationships: *Happy Together,* by Suzann Pileggi and James Pawelski (New York: Tarcherperigee, 2018).

General: *30 Days of Character Strengths,* by Jane Anderson (Strength Based Living LLC, 2018).

Project management: *Be a Project Motivator,* by Ruth Pearce (Oakland: Berrett-Koehler, 2018).

Specific character strengths

Creativity: *Wired to Create,* by Scott Barry Kaufman and Carolyn Gregoire (London: Vermilion, 2015).

Curiosity: *Curious?* by Todd Kashdan (New York: Harper, 2009).

Judgment: *Thinking, Fast and Slow,* by Daniel Kahneman (New York: Farrar, Straus and Giroux, 2011).

Love of Learning: *The Power of Mindful Learning,* by Ellen Langer (Boston: Da Capo Lifelong Books, 1997).

Perspective: *Practical Wisdom,* by Barry Schwartz and Kenneth Sharpe (New York: Riverhead Books, 2011).

Bravery: *The Courage Quotient,* by Robert Biswas-Diener (San Francisco: Jossey-Bass, 2011); and *Psychological Courage,* by Daniel Putnam (Lanham, MD: University Press of America, 2004).

Perseverance: *Mindset,* by Carol Dweck (New York: Random House, 2006).

Honesty/Authenticity: *The Gifts of Imperfection,* by Brené Brown (Minneapolis: Hazelden, 2010); and *Authentic,* by Stephen Joseph (London: Piatkus, 2017).

Zest: *The Body and Positive Psychology,* by Kate Hefferon (UK: Open University Press/McGraw Hill Education, 2013).

Love: *Love 2.0,* by Barbara Fredrickson (New York: Hudson Street Press, 2013).

Kindness: *Self-Compassion,* by Kristin Neff (London: Hodder & Stoughton, 2011).

Social Intelligence: *Social Intelligence,* by Daniel Goleman (New York: Bantam Books, 2006).

Teamwork: *Woven,* by Fiona Campbell Hunter (New Zealand: Fiona Campbell Hunter, 2017).

Fairness: *The Fairness Instinct,* by L. Sun (Amherst, NY: Prometheus Books, 2013).

Leadership: *The Humanitarian Leader in Each of Us,* by Frank LaFasto and Carl Larson (Thousand Oaks, CA: Sage Publications, 2012).

Forgiveness: *Beyond Revenge,* by Michael McCullough (San Francisco: Jossey-Bass, 2008).

Humility: *Humility: The Quiet Virtue,* by Everett Worthington (Philadelphia: Templeton Press, 2007).

Prudence: *Organize Your Mind, Organize Your Life,* by Paul Hammerness and Margaret Moore (Don Mills, Ontario: Harlequin, 2011).

Self-Regulation: *Willpower,* by Roy Baumeister and John Tierney (New York: Penguin Press, 2011).

Appreciation of Beauty & Excellence: *Awe,* by Paul Pearsall (Deerfield Beach, FL: Health Communications, 2007).

Gratitude: *Thanks!* by Robert Emmons (Boston: Houghton Mifflin, 2007)

Hope: *Making Hope Happen,* by Shane Lopez (New York: Free Press, 2014).

Humor: *Humor as Survival Training for a Stressed-Out World,* by Paul McGhee (Bloomington, IN: AuthorHouse, 2010).

Spirituality: *The Gospel of Happiness,* by Christopher Kaczor (New York: Image Books, 2015).

APPENDIX:
ABOUT THE VIA INSTITUTE ON CHARACTER

The VIA Institute on Character is a nonprofit organization headquartered in Cincinnati, Ohio. Its mission is to advance the science and practice of character strengths. In the early 2000s, the VIA Institute supported pivotal work on the nature of positive character involving a 3-year study by 55 scientists led by Christopher Peterson and Martin Seligman and culminating to the landmark text *Character Strengths and Virtues: A Handbook and Classification.* The project also involved the creation of two valid and free measurement tools—the VIA Inventory of Strengths (colloquially known as the VIA Survey) for adults, and the VIA Youth Survey. The VIA Institute had been supported generously by the Manuel D. and Rhoda Mayerson Foundation.

A handful of the central activities currently include:

- Creating and validating measures of character, developing practical tools for individuals and practitioners, and educating people about character strengths.
- Supporting hundreds of researchers every year to use character strengths questionnaires in basic and applied science.
- Giving keynotes and workshops on character strengths to thousands of practitioners and consumers each year.
- Offering practical resources on the website, which is visited by someone every 5 seconds of every minute of each day.
- Partnering with global leaders in business, education, technology, coaching, and other fields to help advance VIA's mission.

A substantial portion of all VIA revenue from reports, courses, and partnerships supports new research in the science of character each year.

Visit the VIA Institute at its website: www.viacharacter.org.

THE SCIENCE OF CHARACTER, THE PRACTICE OF WELL-BEING

Fuel Your Strengths Journey with these resources that you can find at www.VIACharacter.org:

 VIA In-Depth Profile Reports: In-depth, personalized profiles based on your survey results.

 VIA Courses: Online classes for both personal and professional strengths development.

 Strengths-based Panda Planner: Infuse your strengths into your daily tasks and goals.

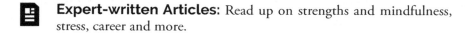 **Expert-written Articles:** Read up on strengths and mindfulness, stress, career and more.

VIACharacter.org

INSTITUTE ON
CHARACTER